jhp

Gourmet Guide

with over
60
Signature
recipes

2016/2017 Gourmet Guide RATED

Contents

*"Food for the body is not enough.
There must be food for the soul."*

DOROTHY DAY

Foreword

I believe that teaching is very similar to gardening, except that you are working with people, not plants. Many past students have matured into beautiful productive trees.

Jenny Handley was one of our 'bright stars' at the Cape Technikon, where I was senior lecturer during the seventies and early eighties, and I have followed her career with pride. Her love of the culinary arts is firmly grounded on sound technical knowledge and an understanding of nutrition.

A thirst for knowledge, the opportunity to travel and a drive for continuous improvement are all reasons for her success in the food world.

One can trust her judgement and honest, unbiased recommendations. In South Africa we have outstanding agricultural produce and a long heritage of warm hospitality, grounded in an interesting culture of international food fusion.

This book is an excellent guide to obtaining an overview of this exciting and ever-evolving landscape.

Ina Paarman

Ina Paarman
Cape Town
2016

"For a teacher there is no greater joy and pride than to see one's students reach the peak of their chosen career and become one's equal."

Raymond Blanc OBE

Quickfinder: Restaurants

Quickfinder: Recipes

"One should eat to live, not live to eat."

Molière

Introduction

Do you travel on your taste buds?

Welcome to the inaugural *JHP Gourmet Guide*™ of South Africa, a book that will lead you on a culinary journey from big cities to small towns. Wherever you go you will be able to plan, using the maps as well as recommendations by professional palates and personalities, and link directly to a restaurant website by using your smart phone and the QR code provided.

We live in a time of an explosion of awareness of good food, and are lucky to live in a land where we are exposed to produce and places that feed our appetite for flavour and excellence daily. Restaurants are a social platform and an economic trigger. They are where we come together to celebrate life. Many people who can afford to eat out do so regularly, and label themselves a foodie, gastronome, epicure, gourmet, connoisseur or simply a food-lover.
I cannot imagine a life well lived without being one!

Jenny with Raymond Blanc

So how did we hit a century?

We had to be very discerning in inviting nominations for restaurants to be reviewed in order to produce a list of 100. Foodies provided their nominations for restaurants to be evaluated and applauded. We asked them where they choose to eat, and why. Chefs, too, you will notice, have been asked where they choose to eat - many of them say at home, preferably at the braai! It was once we had the list that a team of professional gourmets - those who are qualified and have experience coupled with credibility - were then approached to evaluate the list of nominated restaurants. The visits to the restaurants were anonymous, and inspections were conducted quietly. The team were selected because they understand provenance and ingredients, seasonality and sustainability, they can distinguish between complexity and simplicity, can interpret balance of taste, texture and acidity in addition to simply appreciating visual splendour and flavour on a plate. Most importantly, they had to understand confidentiality and could be impartial. They will remain so in order to be evaluators for future guides.

Once the restaurant had met the criteria, then the final visit was often announced, to meet and interview the chef, if it had not been done before. We tried to avoid chain restaurants, but in certain instances a restaurant was good enough to be evaluated and met the criteria. Mention is then made of the sister restaurants, but they are not rated and plated.

How did the quest begin?

I travel on my taste buds and find that the best way to unlock and understand a culture is through food. I have spent the last decade visiting restaurants and meeting lauded chefs, from Raymond Blanc of the Belmond Le Manoir aux Quat'Saisons to Michel Roux Jr at Le Gavroche in London, and many in between. Scouring markets from east to west, north to south, I have been on a quest to understand countries and their provenance and found that there is no better than ours. I've asked questions in kitchens, bars, bistros and on the streets to uncover what it is people look for in a restaurant. How do they rate the experience, how much is food and how much is

I interviewed chefs and patrons, owners and locals, published writers and bloggers. They were generous in their giving of information. Coming home I would be reminded that many of our chefs can hold their own anywhere in the world. It is time for them to stand up and own their place on the global gourmet stage. The privilege of compiling this guide has been in meeting our chefs at home.

So what's your favourite restaurant?

I am constantly asked, 'So what's your favourite restaurant?' Well this depends on whether I am looking to celebrate a special occasion, if I want a wind-down Friday night meal with equal emphasis on the food and drink, or if I'm looking for an epicurean adventure. While one often wants to experience the talent of top chefs and fine dining, one cannot do that daily. Gourmet food can be found in cafés and kitchens, or sitting on a street. White linen is not part of every memorable meal, but well-prepared food that starts with the finest ingredients is. A restaurant in a beautiful setting initially impresses a guest. The guest is more susceptible to a good experience in the winelands, the countryside or somewhere with a view of the sea. Restaurateurs in a shopping centre or car park sometimes have to work a little harder to win a diner over. We have taken that into consideration, and made a special effort to visit restaurants all over the country, not just in the Western Cape where interviewees say they holiday in order to visit special restaurants. We have also taken the business traveller into consideration - someone who may want really good food between meetings, or to entertain clients in an appropriate setting. There are others that will lure you further afield - read on!

Jenny with Christian Bodguel

What were the criteria?

A list of 32 criteria was considered with each inclusion. The criteria covered more than food, wine, service, setting, ambience and decor. Restaurants and chefs need to be confident in what they offer and who they appeal to. We questioned ethos regarding seasonality, responsibility, sustainability. We looked at the quality of ingredients, techniques, creativity and consistency. Cleanliness was also scrutinised. We ensured that establishments had survived a season, or two, or many, so that they could be evaluated on consistency. It is interesting to note how many chefs commented on health and wellbeing, living off the land and the use of natural, organic ingredients preferably sourced nearby, from local suppliers, thereby decreasing their carbon footprint and supporting those in their community. You will see that there is little mention of pricing. Value is a personal perception, and those who favour fine dining often seem to throw caution to the wind! It is best to visit a website to check on updated prices and to see if you find them palatable. There is also little emphasis on wine as we believe that is a guide all on its own, and there are many reputable ones.

How have we ensured credibility?

There has been no cost for restaurants to be included, nor are there any hotel or restaurant advertisements, ensuring that this guide is authentic, credible, neutral and not weighted in any way by commercial activity or support.

Chefs will come and go, but their legacy lives on in the recipes they created while there. Try them and enjoy them. Some are intimidating, others easy. Some you will read and admire, others you will test. We have allowed the chefs to share their recipes as they have written them, so be forgiving when you notice that they have not been standardised into a particular format; instead they remain original.

Some chefs, because this is breaking new ground, declined inclusion - we hope to see them next time.

What is the plating rating?

This year there were two categories in which restaurants were awarded their plates:

One plate

Excellent cuisine - a top-quality eating experience

Two plates

Exceptional destination dining - extraordinary cuisine that warrants a special trip

Next year these restaurants will be evaluated again in terms of all criteria, but with a greater emphasis on consistency, and those coming out tops will be awarded their third plate. The other inclusions are for memorable meals - worth trying for good quality, original cuisine if you are in the area.

What do you think?

As this is the first *JHP Gourmet Guide*™, we would like your feedback and comments. It will be produced annually. You, too, can nominate your favourite restaurant. Visit www.jennyhandley.co.za and complete a nomination form.

Jenny Handley, curator and writer

Jenny with Chantel Dartnall

"You learn to cook so that you don't have to be a slave to recipes. You get what's in season and you know what to do with it."

JULIA CHILD

Thanks

Whilst the guide covers from haute cuisine to hot-and-happening, my thanks are truly from the heart. This Gourmet Guide™ would not have been possible without inspiration from renowned chefs globally who made me realise that their SA counterparts are as good. There are many others who need to be thanked:

· The many foodies, locals and visitors, who graciously allowed me to interrogate them about where they eat out, and why.

· The professional gourmet team who came on board so readily, who understood the responsibility in evaluating the restaurants. Remain anonymous - we want you back next year!

· Friends and family who accompanied me, far and away (very willingly!), to visit the restaurants.

· The talented chefs who accommodated us often at very busy times, and always so professionally.

· The marketing teams at restaurants, PR companies and consultants who nagged chefs on our behalf for photographs and recipes.

· Ina Paarman, for writing a personal endorsement for this guide, and for originally inspiring my culinary journey when I was a student.

· John Loubser and Drew Sherwood and the the Map Studio team for embracing the concept and being supportive and flexible.

· Thea Grobbelaar for her invaluable editing.

· To my colleagues in this industry who have been with me every step of the way - you know who you are and you know how much I appreciate your support.

· Natalie Brock, right hand, sounding board and the ringmaster of the circus.

It's not just fine dining. It's where to find food that stands out, something special. We hope that there is something to whet everyone's appetite.

The Restaurants

5 Rooms

cosmopolitan cuisine in the Cape Winelands

The Alphen Estate,
Alphen Drive,
Constantia, 7806
+27 21 795 6313
www.alphen.co.za/5rooms
GPS: S34°00'42.29"
E18°27'04.82"

The Alphen boutique hotel on the leafy Constantia wine route provides welcome respite, with privacy and style, on a historical estate. It was once a wine estate, then a working farm and still sports an old mill. Popular with business and leisure travellers alike, their signature restaurant, 5 Rooms, offers just that – five private and stylish rooms that are well frequented by couples looking for subdued elegance, or parties who want the privacy of their very own room. White linen-covered tables lend a touch of elegance and grace, and there is service to match.

After drinks on the terrace or at the popular Rose Bar, you will be invited to move to your 'room'. In winter there are crackling log fires to warm you. The menu is simple and sufficient, not fancy fine dining, and there truly is something for everyone. Regulars rave about the spicy calamari starter, and the chips fried in duck fat as an accompaniment to their meat, fish and poultry mains.

For a less formal option there is La Belle Bistro & Bakery next door, where salads and sandwiches and other light meals are up for grabs. Wooden chairs and tables outside on the terrace and sufficient shade make this first choice in the hot summer months.

9th Avenue Bistro

robust and reasonable bistro fare

2 Avonmore Centre, 9th Avenue,
Morningside, Durban, 4001
+27 31 312 9134
www.9thavenuebistro.co.za
GPS: S29°50'11.63"
E31°00'50.35"

Since 2001, in the simple setting of a car park in 9th Avenue, Graham and Gina Nielsen's bistronomy has been a favourite among Durbanites with robust appetites. The Nielsens waitered together, travelled together and then decided to open up shop together. Graham, a philosopher, found his niche in the kitchen, and Gina, a trained teacher, manages front of house. They have been joined by head chef Charlie Lakin who hails from Yorkshire with a Michelin Rising Star award under his belt. Regular dishes remain on the menu, but their 10-course tasting menu (to be booked in advance) gives Charlie space to play and show his love of foraging.

The ambience is relaxed. Portions and flavours are generous and staff are friendly and helpful. The team has produced a list of their favourite restaurants that range from café to casual, drinking and dancing spots to fine dining and, of course, a list of great curry spots, to give to guests from out of town. They have also created a wide and pleasing wine and beverage list. Their signature dish is the pear, walnut and blue cheese salad, perfect for the hot, humid climate.

The Nielsens recently opened the Boiler Room, a canteen for office workers in the heritage building that housed the old Lion Match factory. Here they plan to have pop-up themed nights that will allow them to reminisce and provide their faithful followers some tastes of their travels.

INGREDIENTS

Chocolate sorbet

2 cups water
3/4 cup sugar
1/2 cup cocoa powder (preferably Dutch Process)
1 1/2 teaspoons instant espresso powder
1 teaspoon vanilla extract

Soufflé base

500g mango purée (use 3–4 mangoes)
250g castor sugar
30g cornflour
juice of 1 lemon

Assembly

softened butter for greasing and extra castor sugar
3 egg whites
35g castor sugar
150g soufflé base

METHOD

Chocolate sorbet

Whisk first three ingredients in heavy-based medium-sized saucepan over medium to high heat until sugar dissolves and mixture come to a boil. Stir in the espresso powder and vanilla. Chill. Transfer the mixture to an ice-cream maker and process according to the manufacturer's instructions. Transfer sorbet to container and freeze until firm. Can be prepared up to three days in advance.

Soufflé base

Peel and remove flesh from the mangoes. Purée the flesh and weigh out 500g. Heat the castor sugar, cornflour and lemon juice in a pan and whisk together until it thickens, stirring all the time. Remove from heat, add purée and leave to cool.

ASSEMBLY

Grease the soufflé dishes with butter, using a pastry brush, with upward and well-measured strokes to ensure an even rise, then dust with castor sugar. Whisk the egg whites until soft peaks form. Add the castor sugar and whip again until soft and firm. Gently fold the egg whites into the soufflé base until all has been incorporated and is smooth. Fill the soufflé dishes with the mixture, flatten the top with a palette knife and run your finger around the rim to help the rise. This can be done up to three hours in advance, if stored in a fridge. Preheat the oven to 200°C and cook the soufflé for 10 minutes. When well risen, serve immediately with a scoop of chocolate sorbet.
Serves 4

Mango soufflé with chocolate sorbet

95 Keerom

simple, real simple - less is more

95 Keerom Street,
Cape Town City Centre,
Cape Town, 8001
+27 21 422 0765
www.95keerom.com
GPS: S33°55'35.39"
E 18°24'57.10"

In Cape Town's city centre, a mere hop and skip from the judicial chambers, sits this heritage building that was part of the original Company Gardens, now chic and modern. The ambience, in spite of being frequented by so many business people, is relaxed and, by night, romantic. The service is slick and quick if you want it or more leisurely if you have time. Either way you are guaranteed to experience chef patron Giorgio Nava's authentic Milanese cuisine using the best of local and imported ingredients.

Giorgio, who has lived in South Africa for 15 years, is inspired by his Italian culture. 'We live and think about food all day. It was a gift to grow up in a family of exceptional cooks. Through food and family we share. Italian food is like a bible or dictionary of food. We must give the ingredients the right interpretation. You cannot change a recipe, but you can add a little bit or take a little off; always keep the basis the same.' Chef Nava loves rice and rosemary, and his favourite dish is saffron risotto Milanese.

Long hours (Giorgio also owns Carné SA, well loved by Cape carnivores) and a love of food have paid off. Giorgio won the Pasta World Championships in Parma with his rendition of pasta with broccoli and oregano flowers. Try it and you will see why, or devour his butternut ravioli gently flavoured with sage, but without a doubt finish your feast with Il Fondente al Cioccolato (dark Italian chocolate hot fondant with a liquid chocolate centre) - truly sublime. Their wine list is extensive (with a whiff of expensive), with Italian wines by the glass and a large and reasonably priced grappa selection.

INGREDIENTS

1 head of broccoli, with leaves
100ml extra virgin olive oil
2 cloves garlic, sliced
6 anchovies
4 slices stale bread, cut into cubes
salt and pepper
320g Barilla cavatelli or short pasta
4 or 5 sun-dried tomatoes
fresh oregano flowers

METHOD

Boil the broccoli and leaves in salted water. When soft, place in salted ice water to stop it from cooking and to maintain a beautiful green colour. Reserve the cooking water.

Heat some of the olive oil in a frying pan with the sliced garlic and four anchovies. Stir until melted.

Remove the garlic and add the bread cubes. Fry until crispy.

Blend the broccoli (except the leaves) with the remaining two anchovies, olive oil, salt and pepper until soft and creamy; add some of the broccoli cooking water if necessary. Place this cream in the frying pan with the bread.

Cook the pasta in the remaining broccoli cooking water until al dente. Drain the pasta and mix gently with the broccoli cream for one minute.

Place the broccoli leaves in a pasta bowl and then add the pasta. Top this with thinly sliced dried tomatoes, bread cubes and oregano flowers before serving.

"Italian food is like a bible or dictionary of food. We must give the ingredients the right interpretation."

CHEF GIORGIO NAVA

Cavatelli pasta with a broccoli velvet sauce and oregano flowers

AtholPlace

finely tuned flavours in a four-course feast

"We like to serve clean, flavourful food with varied influences."

90 Pretoria Avenue,
Atholl, Johannesburg, 2196
+27 11 783 3410
www.morukuru.com
GPS: S26°06'42.47"
E 28°03'50.19"

"Sustainability and seasonality are profoundly important to the restaurant's culinary team..."

This Relais & Châteaux boutique hotel knows how to pull out all the stops to make you feel special. Intimate and sophisticated, tucked away from the city beat of Jozi yet close to Sandton, it is serene with tropical greenery and a terrace that extends from the restaurant overlooking the pool. Exclusivity, privacy and discreet security are all guaranteed, as is personal service. The nine large and airy rooms are decorated with exceptional attention to detail. It was formerly the home of decorator Sumari Krige, and she was commissioned to renovate and decorate the property for the Morukuru family. Contemporary decor with a subtle African flavour and a warm home-from-home welcome makes this place perfect for the discerning guest who wants a small environment without sacrificing big needs.

Those desiring extra privacy choose the villa, while more sociable guests gather in the bar for an aperitif and canapés before experiencing innovative and eclectic cuisine with a hint of Asian influence. Sustainability and seasonality are profoundly important to the restaurant's culinary team, and this is reflected in the freshness of flavours. 'We like to serve clean, flavourful food with varied influences.'

The four-course fine dining menu, with a choice of two main courses, changes regularly, and guests are encouraged to state their preferences – if they want a gourmet sandwich instead, that is what they will get. Hope that when you get there the pumpkin and ginger soup is on the menu, or the sea bass, or simply ask for it. The breakfasts are gourmet, beautifully presented and a great option for a private business meeting. Open to the public, with reservations, this 24-seater restaurant aims to please.

INGREDIENTS

Duck breast

1 duck breast, with skin
seasoning of your choice

Pasta

1kg flour
11 eggs
pinch of salt

Spinach and ricotta filling

1 onion, finely chopped
2 cloves garlic, chopped
500g spinach, chopped
250g ricotta cheese
salt and pepper

Hazelnut brittle

1 cup sugar
1 cup hazelnuts (skins removed), toasted

Carrot and star anise purée

500g chopped carrots
1 cup cream
2 cups milk
4 star anise
salt and pepper

Pine nut jus

1 litre rich beef stock
50ml port
30g toasted pine nuts
salt and pepper

Parmesan foam

250g grated Parmesan cheese
500ml mirepoix-infused milk
5ml soy lecithin

Garnish

edible flowers
pea shoots

METHOD

Duck breast

Score the skin of the duck. In a hot frying pan over low heat, place the duck breast skin side down and let it cook slowly. Low heat ensures that the skin goes evenly crispy and takes all the fat out. The breast will be loose from the surface when it is ready. If it sticks, it's not crispy yet. Turn over the breast. The skin should be crispy and golden in colour now. Cook the breast for another four minutes or so to get it to the medium stage. Season to taste. Remove from heat and leave to rest on kitchen towels.

Pasta

Blend ingredients together until just mixed, work dough into a smooth ball, wrap with clingwrap and allow to rest in the fridge for an hour.

Spinach and ricotta filling

Fry onion and garlic until lightly browned, add chopped spinach and sauté over low heat until spinach is cooked and all moisture evaporated. Allow to cool, add the ricotta and chop the mixture until smooth. Season to taste.

To make the ravioli

Using a pasta machine at the second thinnest setting, roll the pasta out into a long strip. Cut this strip in half. Place one strip of the pasta on a floured surface and place tea-spoons of the filling in the middle of the pasta strip, spaced two fingers apart and lining them up. Dampen the pasta around the filling, using a pastry brush (or just your finger) and water. Place the second strip of pasta over the strip with the filling, pressing down around the filling to seal it in. If it sticks, dust with flour. Using a round cookie cutter that is just bigger than the teaspoons of filling, cut out the raviolis and place on a floured tray. Cook the raviolis in a saucepan of salted boiling water until done.

Hazelnut brittle

Melt sugar over low heat until golden brown caramel. Place the nuts on silicon mat and pour over the melted sugar. Once cooled, place it in the food processor and pulse until soil-like consistency is achieved.

Carrot and star anise purée

Place all the ingredients in a deep saucepan, making sure the carrots are covered, and simmer for 20 minutes until the liquid has reduced. Remove the star anise and place the carrot mixture in the blender. Blend until it is very smooth. Season to taste and blitz for a few more seconds. Strain through a chinois or a fine sieve.

Pine nut jus

Reduce beef stock and port together until it coats the back of a spoon. Add the pine nuts, and check seasoning.

Parmesan foam

Heat the Parmesan and milk together in a saucepan. Add the soy lecithin, and blend with a hand blender until it is firm. Froth forms at the top of the liquid.

PLATING

Start with three dollops of the purée on the plate in a triangular shape. Next, place two raviolis alongside two of the dollops of purée. Cut the duck breast at an angle so that you get four triangular shapes out of it. Place two of the duck pieces next to the raviolis. Heat up the foam just until it steams and place it on top of the ravioli. Place the brittle as a dust in between the other components and finish with a little pine nut jus. Lastly, garnish with edible flowers and pea shoots.

Pan-fried duck breast, spinach and ricotta ravioli, hazelnut brittle, carrot and star anise purée, pine nut jus and Parmesan foam

Aubergine

timeless taste sensations from the past to the present

"...the contrast of old and new is seen in the decor and on the plate."

39 Barnet Street,
Gardens, Cape Town, 8001
+27 21 465 0000
www.aubergine.co.za
GPS: S33°55′55.84″
E18°24′57.98″

Tucked away in a little side street of Gardens, authentic and unpretentious, timeless rather than trendy, Aubergine has been impressing diners for 20 years. A mix of local and international fans and well-deserved awards have kept German chef patron Harald Bresselschmidt ambitious and inspired. This historic house, circa 1830, former home of the first Chief Justice of the Cape, allows guests to dine alfresco on the terrace in summer, and to enjoy the intimate ambience indoors in winter. Auslese is Aubergine's function venue, situated nearby in Hope Street.

Classically trained Harald's food and wine pairings are legendary; he has a level of innovation and integrity that makes his cuisine memorable. It is not just about flavour – here pink prawns may be blended with a rosé wine. 'Food must allow the wine to shine, and the wine must allow the food to shine. I cook behind the wine.'

They have their own range of wines to complement their exemplary cuisine. It is obvious that the extensive, impressive wine list has been carefully crafted by a connoisseur, premium wines hand-picked from all over the globe and showcased in a glass corridor. Expensive but worth it. You are sure to enjoy the informative, slick, well-timed service of perfectly presented, fine food that gently rests on a foundation of classics served at century-old tables. Traditional as well as modern, the contrast of old and new is seen in the decor and on the plate. Harald is a master of gastronomy. 'I cook from the ground up. I love vegetables, and we grow our own on a farm in Stellenbosch, sufficient to supply some top restaurants in addition to ours. Growing up on a farm and working the land from the age of six has given me a great appreciation for good quality produce.' There is a pleasing blend of South African produce enhanced by oriental spices. If you are feeling flush, you can add caviar as a treat.

'Creativity is born from authenticity, but is supported by tradition and experience. There is a fine line separating a creative dish from one that is over the top. For me, in a successful dish no one flavour overwhelms another, but rather they co-exist harmoniously and complement each other.'

Harald's favourite restaurants include Nobu and Mosaic.

Aubergine offers a three-, four- or five-course menu with wine pairing. One of the standout dishes is the saffron-flavoured Cape Sea Harvest soup with fried prawns on baby spinach. Of course, the aubergine soufflé, too, is memorable.

INGREDIENTS

Risotto nero

25g butter
1 small onion, chopped
80g Arborio risotto rice
1 sachet squid ink
100ml white wine
250ml vegetable stock
salt and pepper
1 bay leaf
1 teaspoon chopped fresh oregano
2 tablespoons chopped fresh parsley
40g cold butter

Pan-seared abalone

30g butter, melted
4 fresh abalone
½ teaspoon salt flakes
zest and juice of 2 limes

METHOD

Risotto nero

Heat butter in a deep saucepan and sweat the onion until soft. Add the risotto rice, stir for a few seconds to heat up the rice, add the squid ink and deglaze with the white wine. Reduce until dry, then add one-third of the vegetable stock, season and cook on high heat while stirring continuously. Add more stock as the rice cooks just about dry. This process should take 11–13 minutes. Add the herbs and butter and stir until integrated. Adjust with stock if necessary, to make sure the risotto stays moist while binding it with the butter.

Pan-seared abalone

Melt butter in a frying pan and sear the abalone, adding the salt and lime zest and juice to finish. Remove from the heat and serve immediately with the risotto.
Serves 4 as a starter.

WINE PAIRING

Dornier Donatus White, or David Sadie Grenache if red is preferred.

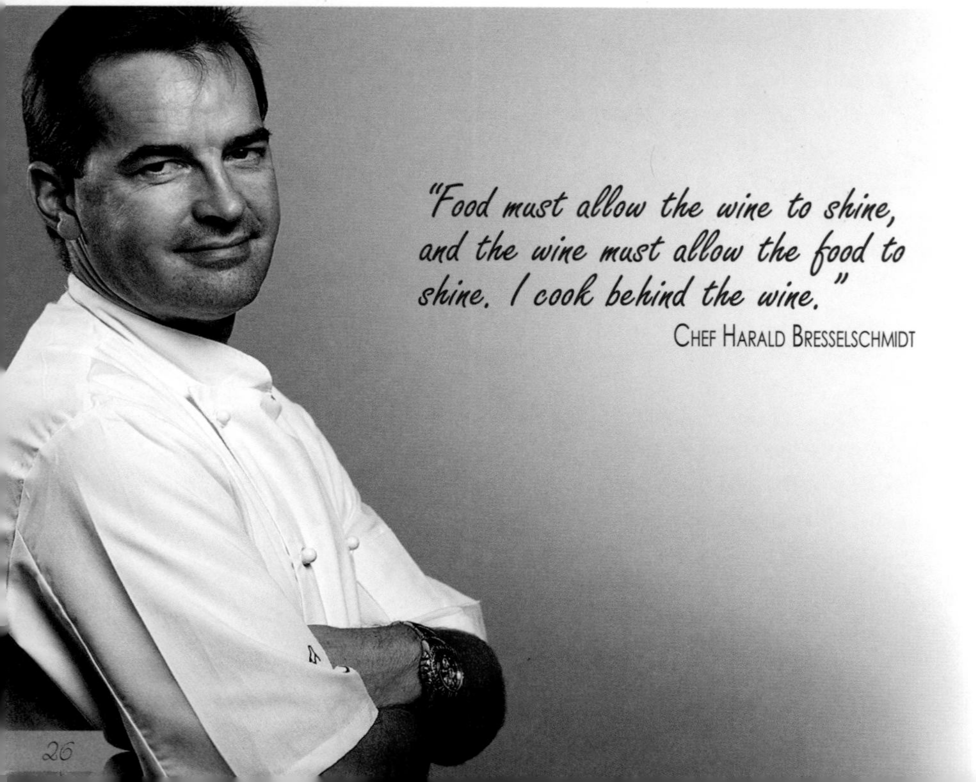

"Food must allow the wine to shine, and the wine must allow the food to shine. I cook behind the wine."

CHEF HARALD BRESSELSCHMIDT

Abalone, pan-seared and served with risotto nero

Azure Restaurant

modern South African cuisine with Asian and French influences

"...culinary talent is obvious in the local specialities and international classics that please both South African and visiting diners..."

Halfway between cosmopolitan Camps Bay and its sleepier sister Hout Bay, the private setting of the Twelve Apostles, with its panoramic views of the Atlantic Ocean, makes it perfect for a special occasion or getaway. The decor of the restaurant is obviously nautical and, not surprisingly, blue. Wind down in the spa, have drinks in the Leopard Bar or enjoy a sundowner on the deck before savouring chef Christo Pretorius's fresh, seasonal produce, perfectly presented. He strives for perfection and loves the privilege of working with produce that holds its own globally. Christo and his wife, also a chef, find inspiration by travelling 'to eat and drink whatever we can get our hands on, to experience different textures and flavours'. His favourite ingredients are Asian - saké, rice vinegar, mirin, limes, ginger and lemongrass. You will find these in his legendary pickles. 'Seasonality and sustainability rule my kitchen in every respect. It should be the norm for all chefs.'

Victoria Road, Camps Bay, Cape Town, 8005
+27 21 437 9029
www.12apostleshotel.com/food-and-drink/azure-restaurant
GPS: S33°59'01.19" E18°21'30.34"

He exhausts innovation with skill and passion when it comes to his seafood - treat yourself to his 'Taste of the Sea' menu, or the equivalent vegetarian menu. Christo's food and wine pairings are the result of his instinct and the insights of renowned sommelier Gregory Mutambe, who has produced an impressive wine list. Chef recommends their prawn dhal and the baby calamari risotto with cauliflower and a calamari broth. Finish off with 'When life gives you lemons' - a lemon crème and poppy seed cake. Plates are an exhibition of visual splendour (equivalent to the art collection in the hotel) and culinary talent is obvious in the local specialities and international classics that please both South African and visiting diners, as does the friendly and refined service.

Christo's ultimate food? A braai with his wife, baby girl and friends - 'Nothing beats a great braai with lots of meat, beer and *braaibroodjies*!'

Prawn dhal (recipe overleaf)

MISE EN PLACE

Sautéed tiger prawns
Cooked lentils
Lentil curry
Celeriac and apple purée
Pickling liquid
Pickled apple
Pickled cucumber
Cumin yoghurt
Hydrated sultanas
Apple chutney
Marmite butter

INGREDIENTS

Sautéed tiger prawns

200ml olive oil blend
16–20 prawns, cleaned and deveined
100g Marmite butter
40g Khoisan salt
10g black pepper
lemon juice

Cooked lentils

500g Le Puy green lentils
500g yellow lentils
500g brown lentils
2 carrots, peeled
2 white onions, peeled and left whole
2 bay leaves
12 sprigs thyme
10 green peppercorns
3 cloves garlic, crushed

Lentil curry

100g curry powder
60ml turmeric
300g white onions, chopped
45ml olive oil
100g butter
10 cloves garlic, grated
60ml grated ginger
500g Le Puy green lentils, cooked
500g yellow lentils, cooked
500g brown lentils, cooked
2 litres chicken stock
juice and zest of 4 lemons
300g fresh coriander
15g Khoisan salt
10g black pepper
250ml cream

Celeriac and apple purée

200g white onions, thinly sliced
20g garlic
50g butter
1kg celeriac, peeled and thinly sliced
400g apples, peeled and thinly sliced
500ml milk
8g salt
2g white pepper

Pickling liquid

70ml mirin
30ml rice vinegar
10ml lemon juice
100ml sugar
100ml water

Pickled apple

1 apple, brunoise
5g Khoisan salt
2g white pepper
125ml pickling liquid

Pickled cucumber

2 cucumbers, peeled and seeded, brunoise
3g Khoisan salt
2g white pepper
125ml pickling liquid

Cumin yoghurt

500ml plain yoghurt
10g cumin powder, toasted
zest and juice of 1 lemon
5g Khoisan salt
5g white pepper

Hydrated sultanas

400ml apple juice
200g dried sultanas

Apple chutney

150ml white wine vinegar
100g white sugar
50g red onion, brunoise
400g apples, grated
20g red chillies, diced
5g ground cumin
5g ground cinnamon
10g ginger, grated
zest and juice of 2 limes
3 green apples, brunoise

Marmite butter

500g butter, softened
50g Marmite, or to taste

METHOD

Sautéed tiger prawns

Add the oil to a hot, medium-sized frying pan. Add a portion of prawns and sauté for two to three minutes. Add the Marmite butter, salt and pepper. Deglaze with lemon juice.

Cooked lentils

Soak the different lentils separately overnight in cold water. The next day rinse the lentils, place in separate saucepans (they all have different cooking times) and cover with cold water. Bring to the boil, remove from the heat and strain. Place in another saucepan, cover with fresh water and add the carrots, onions, bay leaves, thyme, green peppercorns and crushed garlic. Bring to the boil and simmer for 20–30 minutes, or until the lentils are tender but not split. Drain immediately and spread the lentils on a tray to cool down quickly to room temperature. Remove the herbs and vegetables. Cover and refrigerate for two days.

Lentil curry

Place the curry powder and turmeric in a frying pan and toast to release their natural oils and aroma, making sure that all the spices are toasted. Don't burn. As soon as smoke appears, remove pan from stove. Gently fry the onions in the oil and butter over a medium heat for seven minutes. Sauté until soft and translucent but not brown. Add the grated garlic and ginger and cook until soft. Now add the toasted spices and fry for one minute. Mix in the cooked lentils a little at a time. Add all the stock. If the lentils become too dry, add more stock or water. Once ready to serve, add the lemon juice, zest, chopped coriander, salt, pepper and cream and cook for one minute.

Celeriac and apple purée

In a saucepan, sauté the sliced onions and garlic in butter until translucent. Add the celeriac and apples and sauté with the onions for five minutes. Add the milk, salt and pepper. Cook for 15-20 minutes and test to see if it is soft and tender enough to purée. If not, cook for another five minutes and remove from the heat. Blend to a fine purée and strain through a fine stainless steel mesh sieve. Reheat to order.

Pickling liquid

Combine all the ingredients in a medium-sized saucepan. Bring to the boil and cook until the sugar dissolves. Set aside to cool down before using.

Pickled apple

Place brunoise apple, salt and pepper in a vac pack with the pickling liquid and seal. Remove before service.

Pickled cucumber

Place brunoise cucumber, salt and pepper in pickling liquid.

Cumin yoghurt

Combine all ingredients in the food processor and blend until smooth. Transfer to a squeeze bottle and leave in the fridge ready to be served.

Hydrated sultanas

Pour apple juice over the sultanas and leave to rehydrate for a minimum of one hour.

Apple chutney

Pour the vinegar and sugar into a saucepan and bring to the boil. Add the onion, grated apples, chilliies, spices and ginger. Bring to a simmer and cook for two hours, until the mixture becomes a little thick and glossy. If it becomes too thick, add a little water. When the chutney is ready, add the lime zest, juice and brunoise apple. Allow to cool and store in an airtight container until needed.

Marmite butter

Bring the butter to room temperature. Add the Marmite and whisk until fully combined. Just before serving the prawns, deglaze with the Marmite butter in a hot pan. This adds a great depth of flavour and gives you a massive hit of umami.

ASSEMBLING THE DISH

Heat the lentil curry in a saucepan, being careful not to burn the lentils, and check that the seasoning is perfect. Keep hot, ready for plating. Pan-fry the prawns for two to three minutes, deglaze with the Marmite butter and set aside for plating. Reheat the celeriac purée and set aside for plating.

PLATING

Make sure the plates or bowls are hot. Place a spoonful of the celeriac purée on the plate and smear it into a half-moon shape around the edge of the plate/bowl - or any way you prefer. In the centre of the plate, add a spoonful of the lentil curry, then top with the prawns. Around the lentils and prawns, scatter the pickled apple, hydrated sultanas and pickled cucumber. Squeeze dots of the cumin yogurt around the pickled cucumber and apple. Quenelle the apple chutney on the right-hand side next to the lentils and prawns, and serve.

The kitchen gardens at Babel

Babel

where heaven meets earth on a plate

R45, Simondium, 7670
+27 21 863 3852
www.babylonstoren.com/experience/restaurants/babel
GPS: S33°49'21.02" E18°55'48.08"

The award-winning light and bright restaurant on the Babylonstoren Estate in the Drakenstein Valley serves fresher than fresh. An overnight stay at this luxury rural retreat or a visit to the spa may be added to the menu. At Babel, 'pick, clean and serve' is the ethos; here the garden and kitchen work in harmony. This is a working farm, yet the understated elegance and attention to detail reminds you that it is in a class of its own, as nature intended. Every dish is more than delectable - proof that you do eat with your eyes first. Maranda Engelbrecht is a paragon of creativity who started out in fashion design. 'I get my inspiration from the Babylonstoren gardens; it's a sensory experience of see, touch, hear, smell and taste. Also from seeing flowers that grow into fruit and vegetables. For me it's not only about one ingredient but more about the taste of a composed dish - the balance of sweet, sour, bitter and salt - as well as the visual appeal.' Maranda aims for a balance between healthy and indulgent. 'We have mastered the art of how to optimise seasonal flushes. We have a seasonal theme every month, directed by our garden, that is pulled through all the areas - restaurants, bakery, larder, scented shop, decor, etc.'

Starters are chosen for colour - red, yellow and green - to accommodate the daily pickings. Spot unusual and exotic fruit and vegetables that you may never have tasted before. Mains feature a hero ingredient, harmonised with less dominant companions. Desserts focus on sensory combinations such as sweet and bitter, salt and sweet.

The more casual Greenhouse tea room is housed in a glass conservatory where you can watch the garden grow. Tables are set among the fruit, vegetables and herbs getting some intensive care. Sandwiches, sweet treats and kaleidoscopes of salads served in glass jars form the perfect climax to a guided garden tour.

Maranda's favourite Cape Town restaurants are Hemelhuijs and Hallelujah - and she loves eating with family and friends, at her home or theirs. 'It is through eating that we come together.'

INGREDIENTS

Coconut sorbet

125ml sugar
125ml water
330ml coconut milk
juice of 2 limes

Passion fruit curd

pulp of 11 passion fruits
2 large whole eggs
2 large egg yolks
150g castor sugar
100g butter, melted

Lime salt

zest of 2 limes
50ml Maldon sea salt

Fresh fruit

raspberries
peaches
blueberries
figs
gooseberries
kiwi

Garnish

fresh lemon leaves
rose petals

METHOD

Coconut sorbet

In a small saucepan, bring the sugar and water to the boil, making sure all sugar crystals have dissolved. Once the syrup boils, remove from the heat and set aside to cool completely. Mix the coconut milk and lime juice together. Add the cooled sugar syrup, place in an ice-cream churner and churn until the right consistency is reached.

Passion fruit curd

Place the pulp of the passion fruit in a food processor and pulse until all pips and flesh are loosened up; this will take about 30 seconds. In a mixing bowl, combine the whole eggs, egg yolks and castor sugar. Add the passion fruit pulp and melted butter. Transfer the mixture into a medium-sized saucepan and cook over a very low heat, stirring continuously until the mixture starts to thicken (it should resemble double thick yoghurt). Once the mixture has thickened, remove from the heat and store in sterilised jars.

Lime salt

Place the zest of the limes on a baking tray and dry in the oven at 50°C for 15 minutes. Alternatively, place in a warm place in your kitchen and leave to dry for a few hours. Once the zest has dried, mix the Maldon salt in with the zest.

TO SERVE

Cut the fruit to your liking and place on a plate. Top the fruit with a generous dollop of passion fruit curd. Top the curd with a big scoop of coconut sorbet and sprinkle with lime salt. Garnish with fresh lemon leaves and rose petals.
Serves 6

Passion fruit curd, coconut sorbet and fresh fruit

Bellagio

Mediterranean fine dining influenced by Italy

"Here the emphasis is on seafood, salads and good old-fashioned service."

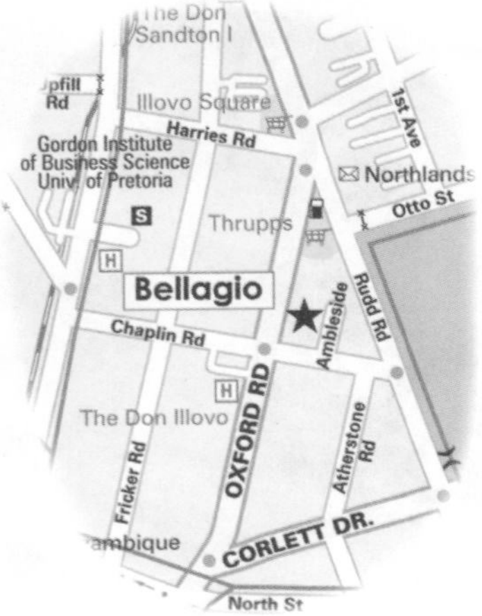

In an uninspiring car park in Illovo sits an inspiring restaurant that draws many regulars. This gem equals the little Italian town called Bellagio on Lake Como in demonstrating the spirit of *la dolce vita*. Here the emphasis is on seafood, salads and good old-fashioned service.

Chef Louise Castle keeps on her toes by reading food and travel magazines and books, and by visiting top restaurants around the world. Her favourite places are, no surprise, Italy and Sardinia, where she adores roaming around food markets in search of her favourite ingredients - basil, garlic and tomatoes. Her favourite dish is crab capellini. In her history of cooking she has always been known for serving simple and unpretentious food, firstly at Ricardo's, then 74 and now Bellagio. Louise is obsessed with quality ingredients. Their specials board changes weekly and the à la carte menu every six months. 'But we have had some dishes on for 20 years!' she proudly claims. All food is seasonally inspired, with more customers wanting 'clean' food - pasta being replaced with vegetables and gluten-free options.

Louise is a fan of Tasha's for casual meals, and for fine dining she loved 500 at the Saxon as her ultimate special occasion restaurant. A meal at Bellagio is best enjoyed with one of their superlative signature cocktails.

Unit 1, Oxford Manor,
196 Oxford Road, Illovo,
Johannesburg, 2196
+27 11 268 0869
GPS: S26°07'53.33"
E28°02'58.22"

INGREDIENTS

queen prawns
squid heads
squid
clams or scallops
kingklip
fresh mussels
1 fennel bulb, finely chopped
½ red onion, finely chopped
cherry tomatoes, finely chopped
red pepper, finely chopped
fresh coriander, finely chopped
1 fresh mild chilli, finely chopped
1 clove garlic, finely chopped
1 teaspoon sumac
coarse pink salt
freshly ground black pepper
olive oil
juice and zest of 1 lime
fresh dill
Italian parsley

METHOD

Grill the prawns, squid, scallops and kingklip (salmon is just as good, or try both). Steam the mussels. Set aside to cool. Add the chopped ingredients and toss. Season with sumac, pink salt and black pepper, and add olive oil and lime zest and juice. Garnish with fresh dill and parsley, and serve with fresh lime wedges.

Bellagio summer seafood salad with lime and fennel

Bistro Sixteen82

contemporary with a touch of class

Steenberg Estate,
Steenberg Road, Tokai,
7945, Cape Town
+27 21 713 2211
www.steenbergfarm.com/bistro1682
GPS: S34°04'30.56"
E18°25'45.95"

Light, bright and airy, this modern restaurant is named after the year in which Steenberg was born. The vineyard and vistas of the stone mountain and indigenous gardens, water features and large terrace provide an enviable setting for breakfast, lunch and tapas. The bistro is famed for its tapas, teamed with Steenberg wines that are not at cellar door prices as the restaurant runs independently of the wine estate.

Kerry Kilpin trained at La Colombe with Frank Devereaux, who whipped her off with him to The Foodbarn when it opened. She describes her role of executive chef as 'bringing the plane in – a chef is air traffic control, but your team is everything. So much goes into the restaurant; it is not just the plate you get. I want you to taste that there is some love put into your food – care and love go a long way.'

The daughter of an Eastern Cape pineapple farmer, Kerry is determined to be true to the ingredients, sourcing from small producers and farmers. Her inspiration comes from seasonal produce, and her strong Thai and other Asian flavours are reminiscent of some of her travels, her North African flavours paying homage to her mentor Frank. Her favourite dish is the Shiraz confit beef with ricotta gnocchi and roasted garlic, and her favourite ingredients are lamb, tuna and asparagus. She, too, loves mentoring young students, giving back to the industry. 'If you are constantly teaching, you are constantly learning.' Although famed for its tapas, this bistro could become famous for Kerry's salted shortbread, treacle apples and popcorn ice cream with caramel sauce.

Delve into the wine shop before you depart, or make a booking for the fine dining restaurant Catharina's at Steenberg, named after Catharina Ras, founder of this, the oldest farm in the country. Or book a four-ball of golf.

INGREDIENTS

Fish

4 x 200g portions of fish of your choice
salt and pepper

Lime vinaigrette

1 teaspoon chopped chilli
1 teaspoon chopped garlic
1 tablespoon grated fresh ginger
125ml canola oil
30ml Tom Yum paste
2g shrimp paste (optional)
80ml freshly squeezed lime or lemon juice
80ml water
100g treacle sugar
10ml fish sauce

Aioli

1 egg
5ml English mustard
10ml red wine vinegar
1 clove garlic, chopped
100ml canola oil
salt

Salad

100g mixed baby salad leaves
50g fresh coriander
30g fresh basil
100g julienned mange tout
4 radishes, finely sliced
100g bean sprouts

Garnish

2 tablespoons toasted sesame seeds
4 sprigs of fresh coriander (optional)

METHOD

Fish

Season the fish with salt and pepper and place in a hot frying pan for about two minutes on each side until fish is golden and cooked through.

Lime vinaigrette

Sauté the chilli, garlic and ginger in a little of the canola oil. Add the Tom Yum paste and shrimp paste and cook for a further two minutes. Add the lime juice, water and sugar and cook for a further five minutes on a low heat. Allow to cool slightly. Place the sauce in a blender and blend, gradually adding the remainder of the oil and the fish sauce. Taste and adjust seasoning if necessary (depending on your taste buds, you may like it a little sweeter, saltier, spicier or sharper).

Aioli

Whisk the egg, mustard, vinegar and garlic in a bowl. Gradually add the oil while mixing continuously to form an emulsion. If you find the mayonnaise getting too thick, add a little water. Season to taste.

Salad

Mix all the leaves, mange tout, radishes and bean sprouts.

TO ASSEMBLE THE DISH

Mix the salad ingredients with a little of the vinaigrette and place on a plate. Place the fish on top of the leaves and then drizzle vinaigrette and aioli over the entire dish. Sprinkle with sesame seeds and garnish with a sprig of coriander.
Serves 4

Asian fish salad

Bistrot Bizerca

innovative, constantly changing, always unique

98 Shortmarket Street,
Cape Town, 8001
+27 21 423 8888
www.bizerca.com
GPS: S33°55′14.71″
E18°25′04.72″

Heritage Square is home to this popular bistro that opens into a cosy cobbled courtyard, idyllic on a balmy evening or sultry summer day. Inside tables, covered in white linen, are backed by a chic brick wall. Here you may witness business by day and the promise of a betrothal by night.

Classically trained French chef Laurent Deslandes may have shed the formality of fine dining, but he has retained the flair, flavour and quality of his homeland. The evidence of his sojourn in Australia, where he and his wife Cyrillia owned and ran fine dining restaurants, is evident. She shops for the freshest and best ingredients at the market, he cooks. They use small suppliers, especially for their organic vegetables. Their beef comes from a farm that has an abattoir on it, and they insist on free-range eggs.

"I think about what goes with what, and then add a little wow factor."
Chef Laurent Deslandes

Attentive service includes the presentation of the chalkboard that denotes the dishes of the day, backed by a small menu of ever-popular dishes. Laurent knows what to play with and what must stay. Wine can be ordered off the predominantly boutique wine list, and by the glass.

Some of the staff have evolved from cleaning to cooking, with Laurent showing them techniques and tips. 'There is always someone behind me, learning, a shadow. After 38 years of this I am still inspired – by ingredients and the weather. I think about what goes with what, and then add a little wow factor. I love artichokes, wild asparagus, broad beans and offal. My food remains classic, generous, fresh and well balanced.'

INGREDIENTS

40g pine nuts
500g Norwegian salmon, the best quality you can lay your hands on
100g rocket or baby greens
80g soft goat's cheese (chevre)
50g pickled ginger, cut into very thin strips
artisanal sourdough bread to serve
lemon wedges (optional)

Dressing

3 tablespoons finely chopped spring onions
100ml extra virgin olive oil
30ml good quality soy sauce

METHOD

Lightly toast the pine nuts in a non-stick frying pan until golden brown. Slice the salmon very thinly, using your sharpest knife. Spread the rocket leaves on a serving platter and arrange the salmon ribbons on top. Roughly crumble the goat's cheese over the salmon and top with the finely sliced pickled ginger.

Mix all the dressing ingredients together and drizzle over the salmon and onto the plate. Scatter the pine nuts and serve with a good quality sourdough bread and lemon wedges (optional).
Serves 4

Norwegian salmon salad

Bombay Brasserie

fine Indian cuisine with silver service

Cape Town's best-kept secret is on the corner of Wale and Adderley streets in the majestic Taj Hotel, which was formerly the Board of Executors building. It is popular with business travellers and those with a discerning palate and appetite for flavour. A sense of opulence pervades the luxurious decor as one settles into comfy armchairs for a memorable edible journey to India. Here the ethos is that everyone should feel like royalty.

Chefs Harpreet Longani and her husband Shyam Longani came from the landmark Taj Mahal Palace Hotel in Mumbai, bringing with them an array of flavours and innovation to open the first restaurant at the Taj at the foot of Table Mountain. In the last seven years Harpreet has procured the best Indian spices and ingredients to ensure consistency, simultaneously embracing all that her new soil has to offer, like game. Working seasonally, Bombay Brasserie caters well for vegetarians, and many a carnivore dines out on the vegetarian food and wine pairing. Here authentic Indian food is served in a contemporary style. The restaurant, decor and presentation may be modern, but the flavours are still pure and basic. 'Everything in our culture revolves around food. It is our passion. I still visit Mumbai annually and our family visit us here. This is my legacy.'

Harpreet's legacy may also lie in her roasted yellow corn soup with turmeric popcorn, her Karoo lamb cubes in saffron curry, or her exceptional Morello cherry baked yoghurt with fennel seed biscotti. You decide.

INGREDIENTS

1 cup oil
6 onions, sliced
1 tablespoon ginger and garlic paste
2 green chillies
2 teaspoons coriander powder
1 teaspoon Deggi Mirch powder
3 tomatoes, sliced
1/2 cup cashew nut paste
2 cups water
1 teaspoon cumin seeds
6 green cardamom pods
2 bay leaves
8 cloves
8 lamb shanks
salt to taste
a few strands of saffron
1/2 teaspoon garam masala powder

To serve

4 potato baskets
4 cups saffron pilaf
4 x 24-carat gold leaves
8 sprigs fresh coriander

METHOD

Heat half the oil in a frying pan and fry the onions until light golden. Add the ginger and garlic paste, green chillies, coriander powder, Deggi Mirch powder and tomatoes. Add cashew nut paste and water and simmer for 20 minutes. Blend to a fine paste and strain. In a heavy-based saucepan, heat the remaining oil and fry the cumin seeds, cardamom pods, bay leaves and cloves. Add the lamb shanks and sear. Add the blended curry and simmer until the shanks are cooked. Season the shanks with salt and finish with roasted saffron strands and garam masala powder. Serve the hot lamb shanks in potato baskets on a bed of saffron pilaf, and garnish with gold leaf and coriander sprigs.
Serves 4

The Taj Hotel,
Wale Street,
Cape Town, 8001
+27 21 819 2000
www.tajcapetown.co.za/dining/bombay-brasserie
GPS: S33°55'28.41"
E18°25'10.98"

Dum ki nalli

Bosman's Restaurant

European cuisine influenced by South African produce

Plantasie Street,
Paarl, 7646
+27 21 863 5100
www.granderoche.com/dining
GPS: S33°45'07.38"
E18°57'35.04"

The Grande Roche is a landmark in Paarl. The 200-year-old property is still turning heads (and tables). Bosman's restaurant may have been around for what feels like forever, over 20 years, but Austrian-born, Michelin-trained executive chef Roland Gorgosilich rings the changes with aplomb. Finesse is not just evident in the food and wine; thoughtful touches are evident everywhere, like the array of reading glasses for diners (acknowledging that those who can afford to eat five-star meals may need assistance to read the menu in soft lighting!). After a glass of Methode Cap Classique from a neighbouring wine farm, you'll be shown to one of 18 beautifully appointed terrace suites that enjoy a sweeping view of the vines. The accommodation is modern, luxurious and pays homage to the history and tradition of the grand old buildings.

If you love gastronomy harmony, this is the place for you. Roland combines local produce with European flair to present an unforgettable gourmet experience. An amuse-bouche will lead you into a variety of dishes that could be seared scallops with blood dumpling nuggets, pork belly, sauerkraut crème, potato-pancetta mousseline and thyme jus, or a truffle-glazed sole cutlet with kohlrabi-pea à la crème, parsley potatoes and white truffle foam may become a firm favourite. A main course could be oven-roasted Chalmar beef fillet with jus-glazed baby cabbage, braised pearl onions, pommes mousseline and oxtail nuggets. Roland's favourite meal is chicken marjoram stew with stewed herb potatoes made by his grandmother. He finds inspiration by speaking to suppliers about new products, and loves to learn about what is new on the market each season. 'I enjoy using local ingredients, combining them with the European flair.' He favours unusual cuts that are not used very often, such as offal – sweetbread and liver feature regularly.

'The menu is product related and therefore changes as fresh ingredients become available. Seasonality is a very important process for a chef, specifically when he writes menus to use the best and freshest products available. Sustainability is important as one has to ensure that ingredients are not exploited, so we try to source products that are farmed and are not on the SASSI list.'

A gourmet destination for locals and visitors with a palate for grace and style.

INGREDIENTS

Avocado crème

1 avocado
1 small red chilli, chopped
20g shallots, chopped
salt and pepper
½ tablespoon olive oil
¼ tablespoon lemon juice
5g fresh coriander, chopped

Spiced carpaccio

12cm-long piece of ostrich
3g thyme
3g rosemary
50g ginger root, chopped

Pepper confit

1 shallot
1 red pepper
1 yellow pepper
2 tablespoons olive oil
1 small sprig thyme
1 small sprig rosemary
1 clove garlic (not more than 5g)
1 tablespoon sweet chilli sauce
salt and pepper
½ tablespoon coriander (preferably fresh)

Seared ostrich fan fillet

50g tandoori paste
5 tablespoons olive oil
300g lean ostrich fan fillet

Seared ostrich fan fillet with avocado crème, spiced carpaccio and pepper confit

METHOD

Avocado crème

Peel the avocado and mash it finely with a fork. Add the chilli and shallots. Season with salt, pepper, olive oil and lemon juice, and add chopped fresh coriander.

Spiced carpaccio

Slice a 12cm-long piece of ostrich. Finely chop the thyme and rosemary, and add chopped ginger root. Roll the ostrich slices in the chopped herbs. Roll up the ostrich, wrap in a piece of clingwrap and then wrap in tinfoil. Place in the freezer for an hour. It must not be frozen too hard – ensure that you can cut it.

Pepper confit

Peel shallot, and peel red and yellow peppers and remove the seeds. Heat olive oil with thyme, rosemary and garlic to 40°C. Place the shallot and peppers in the olive bath. Cook gently at 60–70°C till soft. Remove the shallot and peppers from the olive oil, drain on kitchen towels and chop into fine cubes. Marinate in sweet chilli sauce with salt, pepper and coriander.

Seared ostrich fan fillet

Mix the tandoori paste and olive oil and marinate the ostrich fillet in the mixture for two hours. Remove the ostrich from the marinade and sear it in a hot frying pan on all sides until browned. Cook in a preheated oven at 160°C for four minutes. Remove and allow to rest. Serve with avocado crème, spiced carpaccio and pepper confit.

Bread & Wine

honest, playful and satisfying fare

Take a turn from the culinary mile in Franschhoek onto the family-run and owned Môreson Family Winery. Here you can find a rustic and restful restaurant where you can enjoy Neil Jewell's famous charcuterie served in wooden boxes with fresh breads baked in-house in the Miss Molly deli. Or choose from the two- and three-course lunch menu in Bread & Wine restaurant. 'Neil's Nosh', depending on the season, could include his delicious sweet potato red curry with deep-fried calamari, or a vanilla roasted trout, cauliflower purée with prawn and porcini. His dishes are inventive and the flavours well layered. Presentation is playful. The menus are aimed at those who are prepared to pay slightly more for perfection.

'I gather inspiration from the things I eat, and the thought processes that follow. I don't favour any particular ingredient, as long as it's fresh and local. There is no option other than to follow the seasons. Our menu is a slow-turning wheel, and dishes are swapped out on a regular basis.'

Choose from the Môreson wine list that includes their popular Miss Molly range, named after Môreson's much-loved Weimaraner. There is a petite à la carte menu for kids, created by the younger members of the family. Stock up on wine, charcuterie, preserves and other delicious deli items in the Miss Molly charcuterie. Neil's current favourite dish is the tagliatelle of broad beans, goat's feta and lemon oil. For a casual meal he heads to Boschendal, and for a special treat he heads to Margot Janse's The Tasting Room.

INGREDIENTS

480g pork mince
10 sage leaves, chopped
1 teaspoon salt
3/4 teaspoon sugar
3/4 teaspoon black pepper
1 medium onion, finely chopped
6 large free-range eggs
18 rashers streaky bacon

METHOD

Mix together the mince, sage, salt, sugar, pepper and onion. Divide mince into six balls, and keep refrigerated until needed. Soft-boil the eggs for five minutes. Roll the bacon out between two pieces of clingwrap (this helps to prevent shrinkage). Lay three rashers of bacon onto a piece of clingwrap, top with a ball of meat spread out into a square, and place the shelled soft-boiled egg in the middle. Gently enclose the egg in the meat and bacon. Remove the clingwrap, roll in tinfoil and bake in an oven preheated to 150°C until the internal temperature of the meat reaches 67°C – use a meat thermometer to check. Cool and refrigerate until needed.

Makes 6

Môreson Farm,
Happy Valley Road,
Franschhoek, 7690
+27 21 876 4004
www.moreson.co.za
GPS: S33°53'01.73"
E19°04'19.33"

"I don't favour any particular ingredient, as long as it's fresh and local."

CHEF NEIL JEWELL

Scotch eggs

Bushmans Kloof

innovated and inspired by nature

Blue Mountain,
Clanwilliam, 8135
+27 21 437 9278
www.bushmanskloof.co.za/food-and-drink
GPS: S32°04'25.24"
E19°05'42.04"

On the Rooibos Route that extends from Citrusdal to Clanwilliam, the ultimate spot has to be at Bushmans Kloof Wilderness Reserve & Wellness Retreat, 270km from Cape Town. This Relais & Châteaux property is renowned for top-quality Cape cuisine and indigenous flavours rooted in the bounty of the Cape Floral Kingdom.

This World Heritage site allows you to see Rooibos growing in its natural state. The garden and kitchen teams replicate the concept of companion gardening, working hand-in-hand to ensure that what the chefs need is planted, e.g. edible flowers. Seeds are removed from plants and sown so that the garden is self-sustainable. Citrus fruits such as lemons and limes are used in the restaurant and bar, and transported to sister hotel in the Red Carnation Hotel Collection, the Twelve Apostles Hotel.

Rooibos tea and fynbos find their way to the menu in a myriad ways. High tea, sandwiched in-between a guided rock art walk and sundowner drive to see 36 indigenous species of game, may feature caramel-filled Rooibos cupcakes. Dinner could feature a duo of duck – home-made potted duck ravioli, sesame crusted duck livers with sweetcorn, caramelised pearl onions and a Rooibos oriental dressing. The best way to make room for a Rooibos-inspired dinner is to take a walk in nature, or indulge in their signature Cederberg 'soul'ution treatment at the spa, close to nature in the riverside gazebo. Meals are savoured in The Homestead restaurant, on the pool terrace facing a stretch of rocky cliffs, and in breathtaking outdoor dining venues. The traditional South African braai (barbecue) at Kadoro, a secluded shepherd's cottage, is a favourite.

Rooibos tea is not the only way to quench your thirst. Wine connoisseurs will be pleased with the top wines, some of them from the local Cederberg Cellars, that accompany their gourmet meals.

"Rooibos tea and fynbos find their way to the menu in a myriad ways."

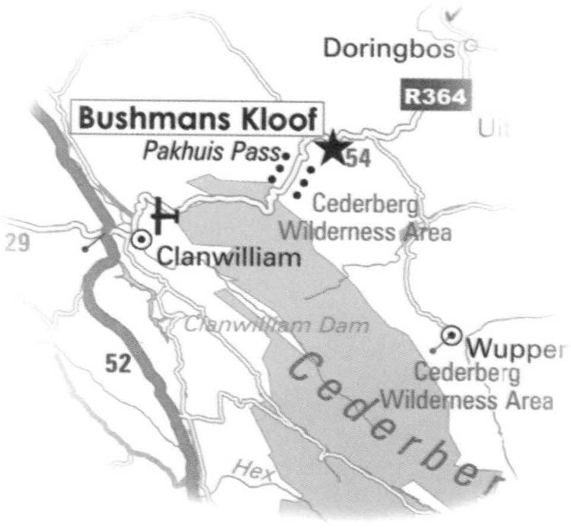

Loin of springbok with Rooibos chocolate oil

INGREDIENTS

Springbok loin

15ml olive oil
2 springbok loins off the bone, trimmed and cut into 6 x 200g portions
salt and pepper

Broccolini

18 sprigs broccolini
2 tablespoons butter

Rooibos chocolate oil

100g bitter chocolate
4 heaped teaspoons cocoa powder
½ teaspoon instant Rooibos tea powder
4 teaspoons peppery olive oil
80ml corn oil

Fondant potatoes

3 medium potatoes
50ml corn oil
2 cloves garlic, halved
100g butter
150ml springbok stock
salt and pepper to taste

Creamed corn

5 large ears corn
4 tablespoons unsalted butter
kosher salt and black pepper

Port jus

200ml port
500ml beef stock
1 sprig fresh thyme

METHOD

Broccolini

Bring a large saucepan of water to the boil and prepare an ice-bath. Blanch the broccolini, then refresh in the iced water. Drain well until ready to serve.

Rooibos chocolate oil

Combine all the ingredients in a mixing bowl and sit it over a pan of warm, not boiling water. Allow to melt, stirring occasionally, then place in a container and keep warm. The mixture will need to be stirred well just before serving.

Fondant potatoes

Preheat the oven to 170°C. Peel the potatoes and cut into slabs about 4cm thick. Using a round pastry cutter, cut the slabs of potato into 5cm circles and trim off the sharp edges. In an ovenproof saucepan, heat the corn oil over medium-high heat. Add the potatoes and garlic and brown the potatoes on one side, taking care not to scorch them. Turn the potatoes over when golden brown and add the butter, stock and seasoning. Bring to a simmer, then transfer to the oven for 12–15 minutes or until the centre of the potatoes is soft. Remove from the oven and leave the potatoes to soak up the butter for 30 minutes. If the stock in the saucepan has evaporated and only butter is left, top up the saucepan with hot water.

Creamed corn

Cut the kernels off three ears of corn. Run them through a juicer, or place them in a blender with a little water and purée. Place the purée and all the liquid into a chinois set over a container. Allow all the corn juice to drain, pressing lightly on the corn but not forcing the purée through the strainer. You should have about half a cup of corn juice. Cut the kernels off the remaining ears of corn. Blanch the corn kernels in lightly salted boiling water for about a minute, skimming off any impurities that float to the surface. Drain the corn and cool in cold water; then drain again and dry the kernels on a paper towel. When ready to serve the springbok, whisk the corn juice in a heavy-based saucepan over medium heat until it thickens; turn down the heat and whisk in the butter. Add the blanched corn kernels and season with salt and pepper.

Port jus

Add the port to a hot saucepan and reduce by half. Add the beef stock and the thyme to the port reduction and reduce over medium heat by two-thirds or until sauce consistency. Remove from heat and strain. Set aside until needed.

TO COMPLETE

Preheat oven to 180°C. Place a large frying pan on the stove over a medium-high heat and add the 15ml olive oil. Season springbok with salt and pepper and place in frying pan. Cook until golden brown. When the meat is sealed, place it on a wire rack over a baking sheet and cook in the oven for four to five minutes, turning occasionally. Test to see if it is done. Meanwhile, drain the potatoes and keep them warm.

When the meat is cooked, remove it from the oven and leave to rest in a warm place for four minutes. Heat the creamed corn and sauté the broccolini in the butter. Dress the plate with the chocolate oil, spoon the broccolini onto the plate with the creamed corn, topped with the fondant potato. Carve the springbok, arrange on the plate and finish the dish off with the port jus.
Serves 6.

Camissa Brasserie

fresh produce and flavours presented simply

Quay 6, Victoria & Alfred Waterfront, Breakwater Boulevard, Cape Town, 8001
+27 21 406 5000
www.suninternational.com/table-bay/restaurants
GPS: S33°54'10.64" E18°25'20.32"

Overlooking Table Bay harbour, with the gentle throb of tugs in the background, the well-known Table Bay Hotel gives one more to appreciate than just the food when dining here. The gracious setting is just a skip away from the Victoria Wharf shopping centre, providing the perfect platform from which to appreciate all the V&A Waterfront has on offer. Chef Jocelyn Myers-Adams' signature dish, Malay curried West Coast lobster pot, is a stand-out, as is her psychedelic-coloured rainbow cheesecake and the not-so-lemon meringue pie, a modern twist on an old classic. Frequented mainly by visitors rather than locals, this is one of Cape Town's secret jewels. Camissa offers sophisticated Cape flavours that keep visitors coming back for seconds, and is starting to lure locals too.

'My inspiration is drawn from the fresh produce that comes with every season, and from local cultural influences. I love the different types of cuisine and use them to enhance dishes. I love all things foraged – edible indigenous flora and fauna. My favourite dish is sautéed soutslaai: dune spinach and wild spinach with farm butter and wild garlic; really delicious! Soutslaai is indigenous vegetation that grows on the sandy coastline. It translates as "sea lettuce" or "sea leaves" and has a dense, salty texture. It is not available by retail; you have to go out and forage for it. We pair this with fresh fish on our Camissa menu.'

There is a strong emphasis on seasonality and sustainability here, and there is a drive to stop buying imported products and to source locally instead. 'We change our menu for each season. Products should be used when they are in season and preserved for use out of season, and we avoid all products that are not produced sustainably, i.e. no fish in the SASSI red category is served.'

In spite of crafting five-star cuisine, Jocelyn is unpretentious and down-to-earth. For a special occasion you may find her dining at The Roundhouse, but for everyday eating she will be at home preparing salads for a braai.

INGREDIENTS

Linefish

5ml olive oil
200g portion of linefish, scaled and pin boned
sea salt
1 lemon

Malay coconut cream and mussel sauce

5g fennel bulb, finely diced
5g carrot, finely diced
10g red onion, finely diced
5g garlic, finely chopped
5g celery, finely diced
5g curry spice mix
3 large fresh mussels, cleaned and steamed
1 cup coconut cream
salt and pepper

Baby marrow spaghetti

120g whole baby marrow
oil
butter
fennel leaves, chopped
salt and pepper

METHOD

Linefish

Heat oil over medium-high heat in pan, season fish with salt and place skin side down in pan. Sear and cook until opaque a third of the way through. Turn the fish and continue cooking until just cooked through. Squeeze lemon over fish – as much as you like.

Malay coconut cream and mussel sauce

Fry the fennel, carrot, onion, garlic, celery and curry spice in a saucepan. Add the steamed mussels, then the coconut cream. Season to taste.

Baby marrow spaghetti

Rinse the marrow, and top and tail. Thinly slice the marrow on a mandoline or a peeler, lengthways, then julienne. Sauté in oil and butter, add chopped fennel and season to taste.

PLATING

In a slightly bowled plate, pour in the coconut cream to about half a centimetre deep. Arrange the three mussels around the edges and place the baby marrow spaghetti in the centre with the fish on top. Garnish to your liking.

Linefish with Malay coconut cream and mussel sauce and baby marrow spaghetti

Camphors

vineyard to plate, pure gourmet pleasure

Lourensford Road, Golden Acre, Somerset West, 7130
+27 21 847 1346
www.vergelegen.co.za/camphors.html
GPS: S34°04'32.51" E18°52'57.39"

Camphors on the Vergelegen Estate is a gourmet destination restaurant grounded by the ancient camphor trees planted in 1700.

The award-winning wines are central to Michael Cooke's food, reflected in interesting components such as port caviar and red wine mayo. In his words: 'Here we have discovered our identity and done something different. We showcase our food through the wine, and the wine through the food.' The sommelier's knowledge and special touches, like a small pot of almond branches brought to the table while enjoying the scallop potjie with apple and almonds, make for an unforgettable meal. The 'tour' menu tells a story and pays homage to the heritage and beauty of the estate, with each dish making sense of the next. Dishes are designed to be enjoyed from light and slight to more substantial, with the menu indicating this. Michael's Forest Floor Flavours, a work of art, was inspired by observing the warm winter colours and falling leaves when he drove into Vergelegen.

He uses produce from the farm and insists that the chefs must understand how it grows. 'Pick it at the right time and you have a premium dish. Too early or too late, these ingredients are wasted.' His menu is a true reflection of provenance. He keeps a diary of the produce, and plans his menu on what happened the previous year. Passionate about the industry and learning, this chef is leading the way and ensures that his chefs leave better than when they came, with elevated skills and knowledge. Cooke's food may be locally sourced, but it is globally influenced.

If you are looking for something more casual during the day in the same heritage setting, try the Stables bistro - classic and contemporary.

"We showcase our food through the wine, and the wine through the food."

CHEF MICHAEL COOKE

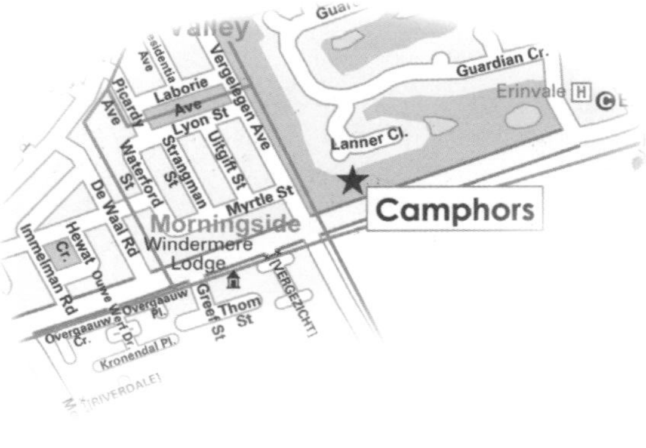

INGREDIENTS

Smoked venison

600g springbok loin, cleaned (yields about 150g per portion)
salt
oat hay

Asian BBQ dressing

90ml plum sauce
30ml rice wine vinegar
15ml fish sauce
100ml soy sauce
20g honey
80g shallots, minced
2 cloves garlic, finely chopped
15g ginger, grated
1 red chilli, chopped
60g sugar

Coconut jellies

1 coconut
1 1/2 gelatine leaves, softened in water

Fennel chutney

10g sugar
3 shallots, sliced
1 fennel bulb, thinly sliced
20ml sherry vinegar
100ml port
250ml water
salt and pepper

Black garlic aioli

2 whole eggs
2 egg yolks
1 teaspoon Dijon mustard
20ml white wine vinegar
150g black garlic cloves, peeled
1 anchovy fillet
500ml grapeseed oil
salt and pepper

Buttermilk dressing

250ml mayonnaise
150ml buttermilk
2 spring onions, sliced
10g parsley, chopped

Garnish

plums, thinly sliced, and some also cubed into tiny blocks
chives, chopped
wood sorrel

METHOD

Smoked venison

Clean the springbok loin of any sinew, and season with salt. Place the oat hay in the bottom of a deep tray, and place a slotted tray over the top, keeping a sufficient space between the two trays. Place the springbok loin into the slotted tray and, using a blowtorch, light the oat hay until it starts smouldering. Cover the slotted tray containing the springbok tightly with tinfoil, and place the trays over an open flame to heat the hay and keep it burning. Leave the trays on the flame for approximately 30 seconds or until the oat hay is smoking sufficiently, and then remove from the flame. Allow to stand for two to three minutes for the springbok to take on the smoky flavour. Remove the tinfoil. Sear the springbok loin in a smoking hot frying pan until sealed on all sides (it must still be rare in the middle). Remove from the frying pan and refrigerate until cold.

Asian BBQ dressing

Combine all the dressing ingredients, except the sugar, in a bowl. Caramelise the sugar in a saucepan. Add all the ingredients to the caramelised sugar in the saucepan (be careful, because it will splatter). Cook until the mixture has thickened and the caramelised sugar has dissolved.

Coconut jellies

Place a strainer over a bowl. Crack the coconut over the strainer, reserving the coconut milk in the bowl. Break the pieces of coconut into smaller pieces and freeze. Prepare a shallow container (deeper than 1cm, and no wider than 6cm) by spraying the inside with non-stick cooking spray. Gently warm 100ml coconut milk in a saucepan, add the softened gelatine and stir to dissolve. Pour the mixture into the prepared tray and refrigerate until set. Once set, turn the tray out onto a cutting board and cut the jelly into 1cm cubes. Refrigerate until required.

Fennel chutney

Caramelise the sugar in a saucepan until golden. Add the shallots and sliced fennel, and sweat until soft. Deglaze with the sherry vinegar and port, and allow to simmer until the alcohol has cooked out. Add the water, turn down the heat to cook very slowly, and simmer gently until soft, stirring occasionally until nearly all the liquid has evaporated. Season to taste.

Black garlic aioli

In a blender, combine the whole eggs, egg yolks, mustard, vinegar, black garlic and anchovy fillet and blend until smooth. With the motor running, slowly pour in the grapeseed oil until the mixture has emulsified. Season to taste.

Buttermilk dressing

Blend all the dressing ingredients together until smooth, and then strain to remove any solids. Season to taste.

PLATING

Thinly slice the seared springbok loin and dress with some of the Asian BBQ dressing. Roll the sliced springbok into cylinders. Place a tablespoon of the buttermilk dressing in the centre of the bowl and arrange the springbok loin on top of the dressing. Mix the tiny cubes of plum with some of the chopped chives and arrange around the sliced springbok, and also gently fold some of the sliced plum in and around the sliced springbok. Place three cubes of the coconut jelly into the bowl with a few dollops of the black garlic aioli. Using two teaspoons, make a quenelle of the fennel chutney and place it neatly in the bowl. Garnish the dish with some wood sorrel or other similar herb, and grate some of the frozen coconut over the top of the dish before serving.

Smoked venison with plums, fennel chutney and coconut jellies

Central One Restaurant

modern comfort food with fresh local ingredients

Radisson Blu Gautrain Hotel,
Corner Rivonia Road and
West Street, Sandton, 2196
+27 11 286 1000
www.radissonblu.com
GPS: S26°06'28.19"
E28°03'31.08"

Central it is. Refined too. For the business or transit traveller, Radisson Blu Gautrain Hotel in Sandton provides easy access to the business district, at the Gautrain station. Having a gourmet meal at Central One is a bonus, as are the sweeping views of this electric city at night. Be sure to grab a window table. Tables are set well apart and that, with the discreet but attentive service, ensures discretion for quiet and confidential conversation. Also perfect for a romantic rendezvous.

"perfect for a romantic rendezvous."

Chef Stuart Cason serves generous portions with liberal flavours. The menu changes seasonally, but the weekly three-course specials menu changes every Tuesday to accommodate regulars and to challenge the creativity of the chefs. 'My inspiration comes from trends and seasonality. Seasonality is important. There is a reason why there is a specific time of year that fruit and vegetables are at their best. So when it's that time of year, why not use them? The culinary world goes through changes in trends. These days peoples' opinions have changed and things that were once new and exciting are outdated. That's just how it is. I kind of like it that way – when things are always changing, it keeps us on our toes and always gets us thinking.'

Stuart believes that nothing beats a good braai – or fresh fish simply cooked, served with a light salad. His seared yellowfin tuna with hummus, olive tapenade, pickled quail egg, slow-roasted cherry tomatoes and Asian greens is a great start to a meal at Central One, as is his smoked duck breast, served with a rich duck liver pâté, cherry gel and duck confit fritters. The winning recipe from the 2014 Inter-hotel challenge (pork belly) and the dish declared the best main course in the 2014 Restaurant Week (the baby chicken) are favourites.

This chef proves on a plate that food is his life, his passion, his everything, apart from his family. He describes his cuisine as fresh ingredients cooked with heart, combining modern and classic cooking techniques. He creates dishes that he enjoys, keeping the guests' palates in mind so that they, too, can enjoy.

INGREDIENTS

whole baby chicken
micro carrots
micro turnips
radishini, halved

Lentil braise

250g lentils
250ml water
1 onion, halved
1 carrot, quartered
knob of butter
5g tomato concasse
5g shimeji mushrooms
1-2 tablespoons red wine jus

Butternut purée

500g butternut, cut into chunks
20g butter
1 tablespoon sugar
salt to taste

METHOD

Baby chicken

Fillet and debone baby chicken. Make sure there are no holes in skin. Take all meat off the skin and place skin neatly back on. Roll in plastic and vacuum pack. Cook in circulator on 72°C for two hours. Remove the chicken from the bag. Grill on all sides or sauté in a frying pan to give the skin a beautiful golden hue.

Lentil braise

Cook lentils in water with onion and carrot. Drain the lentils. Remove the onion and carrot as they were added purely for flavour. On service, sauté the lentils in a knob of butter. Add the tomato concasse and shimeji mushrooms. Finish off with the red wine jus. This will deepen the colour of the braise and add another dimension of flavour. Check for seasoning.

Butternut purée

Place the butternut in a saucepan with the butter, sugar and salt. Pour over just enough water to cover the contents of the saucepan. Cover the saucepan with a cartouche (greaseproof paper, cut or torn to the size of the saucepan with a little tear in the centre to allow steam to escape). Place the saucepan on a medium heat and allow to simmer for 30-45 minutes until the butternut is nicely softened. When cooked, transfer to a blender using a slotted spoon. Reserve the cooking liquid from the butternut as you will need this for blending the purée. Blend to a velvet-smooth purée, adding the reserved liquid. You can add more sugar or salt here depending on your taste.

PLATING

Drop a spoonful of the butternut purée onto a plate. It should hold its shape. Spread the purée into any pattern you desire. Next place a spoonful of lentil braise into the centre of the plate. On top of the lentils place the grilled baby chicken, cut in half or whole if that is preferred. Place the cooked halved baby vegetables around the plate. Drizzle the chicken and lentils with red wine jus and serve.

Baby chicken with lentil braise and butternut purée

Chai-Yo

true tantalising tastes of Thailand

65 Durban Road,
Mowbray, Cape Town,
7700
+27 21 689 6157
www.chaiyomowbray.co.za
GPS: S33°56'55.69"
E18°28'50.26"

Hugging the intersection of two busy roads in Mowbray there is a prominent building, nearly a century old, where Chai-Yo has its home. Meaning 'cheers' in Thai, this relaxed replica of a Thai street café, although indoors, serves bona fide flavours of Thailand in an authentic way.

Decor is simple – the wooden tables and chairs with the ubiquitous blue-and-white Thai crockery that one expects. Portions are of a healthy size, and service is always in true Thai style – unassuming, efficient and pleasing. The menu is extensive (meat, poultry, seafood, noodles and curries), but if overwhelmed by choice, the attentive staff will walk you through your options. There are a few unpredictable items that are worth trying. Standard starters such as spring rolls and tempura vegetables form the basis of a medley that includes the more interesting sweetcorn cakes and calamari on skewers.

The Pla Taud Lard Prik (fried kingklip fillets with a spicy chilli, garlic, lemongrass and basil sauce) and the Angry Duck make a visit to this restaurant worthwhile. Their Chicken Pad Thai is also highly recommended.

Coffee at Chefs Warehouse & Canteen

Chefs Warehouse & Canteen

laid-back fine dining standards in an unpretentious setting

Set in the bustling culinary street of Cape Town, Bree Street, the Chefs Warehouse & Canteen has increased chef Liam Tomlin's large following of devoted fans. It offers an epicurean adventure of note – whet your appetite in the kitchen shop and satisfy it in the laid-back restaurant.

Despite shedding the affectations and refines of fine dining restaurants where he developed his reputation, there are some core principles of being a restaurateur that Liam will never relinquish. Here he replicates the standards set in fine dining, without short cuts, but has the pleasure of doing it all on his own terms in an informal environment. 'Here we are more relaxed and we do not have to stick with one cuisine. We have been able to choose our hours and do not take reservations.' Diners are happy to get there early or queue.

Service is slick and knowledgeable, and the clientele is eclectic and cosmopolitan. The warehouse-feel relaxed dining area is sandwiched between an overflowing emporium of superlative kitchen equipment and recipe books, and the Asian-style street café next door, where the menu changes daily. Treat yourselves to 'tapas for two'. While you savour Liam's tapas, your eyes will be drawn to the wide range of high-quality deli-style ingredients on shelves around you. Rub shoulders with fellow gourmets from all over the world who have come in search of honest, authentic street food.

It may be quick, it may be casual, but Liam's food is always memorable.

92 Bree Street,
Cape Town, 8001
+27 21 422 0128
www.chefswarehouse.co.za
GPS: S33°55′15.04″
E18°25′05.47″

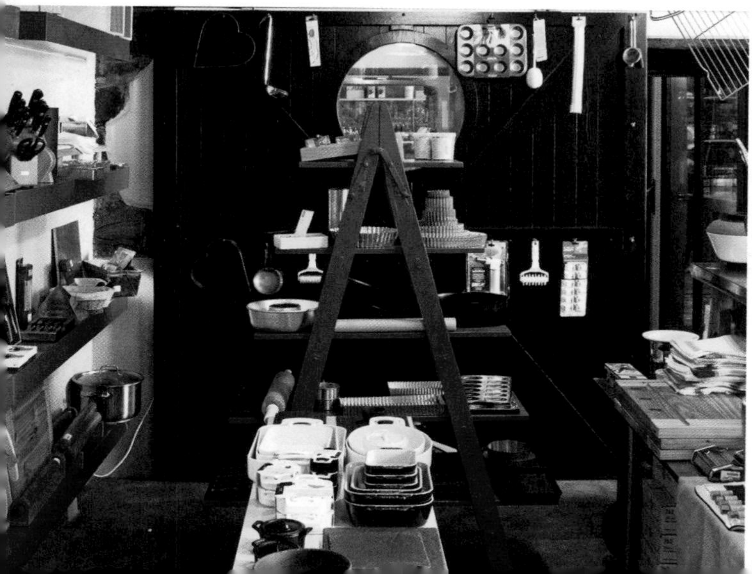

Warm chocolate fondant

INGREDIENTS

20g melted unsalted butter for greasing moulds
castor sugar for lining moulds
200g dark chocolate, finely chopped
200g unsalted butter, softened
200g icing sugar, sifted, plus extra for dusting
4 medium-sized free-range eggs
4 medium-sized free-range egg yolks
55g plain flour
35g good quality cocoa powder

METHOD

Preheat the oven to 190°C. Prepare eight dariole moulds or ramekins by brushing them well with melted butter, using upward strokes around the sides. Chill until firm, then brush again with another layer of butter. Coat the ramekins with castor sugar, shaking out the excess. Place the ramekins on a baking tray and set aside.

Place the chocolate into a stainless steel bowl and set this over a saucepan of simmering water. Stir the chocolate until melted and smooth. Keep warm.

Using an electric mixer, cream the butter and icing sugar together until pale and doubled in volume. Mix the whole eggs and egg yolks together and add them, a little at a time, to the creamed butter and icing sugar, beating well between each addition. Reduce the speed of the mixer and add the melted chocolate. Remove the bowl from the mixer and sift in the flour and cocoa powder, folding them into the chocolate mixture and taking care not to overwork the mixture. Spoon the mixture evenly into the prepared moulds; they should be just over half full. Place in the oven and bake for eight to 10 minutes. After eight minutes, remove one of the fondants and check that it is cooked around the edges and the centre still looks soft. Insert a skewer to test the centre; the skewer should come away warm but the centre should remain liquid. If you think it needs more time, return to the oven for another two minutes.

Remove the fondants from the oven and rest for one minute, then carefully turn each one out onto a serving plate. Dust with icing sugar and serve.
Serves 8

"It offers an epicurean adventure of note..."

Cheyne's

from delicious beginnings to happy endings

Main Road,
Scott Estate, Hout Bay,
Cape Town, 7806
www.cheynemorrisby.com
+27 21 790 3462
GPS: S34°02'40.55"
E18°21'35.43"

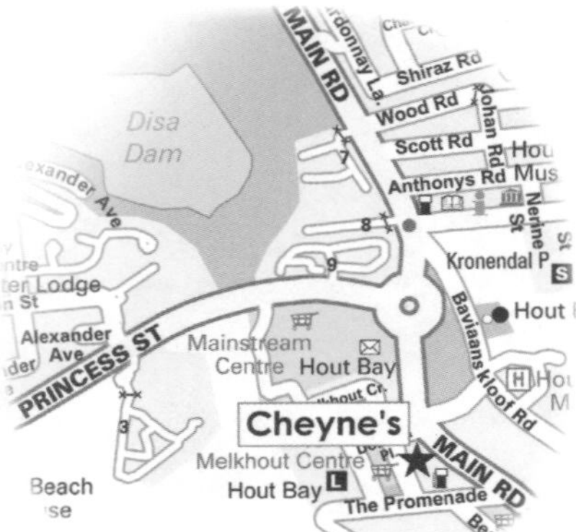

An inconspicuous house on the main road of Hout Bay is the perfect platform for locals and visitors alike to sample small plates of deliciousness in a few interconnected, dark and intimate rooms. The restaurant is named after chef Cheyne Morrisby, who takes you on an Asian journey of intense flavours. The tapas menu is divided into four sections – sea, land, earth and ... happy endings – and all portions are starter size. It is the ideal place to congregate with friends and share as many dishes as possible. Unusual ingredients provide fodder for interesting conversation with the well-informed service staff in this cosy spot. Tastes are exquisite, presentation equally good and if you struggle to make a choice, allow the staff to take the lead in what is sure to be an edgy, interesting ride. While the choice will change, you are sure to see the chilli salt squid and soft-shell crab on the menu. Take a chance on the Tokyo beef slider or the Mumbai chilli beef for some spice. A good happy ending could be the tonka bean dark chocolate fondant with peanut butter ice cream, or a selection of artisanal cheeses.

De Grendel

contemporary cuisine showcasing the Cape

De Grendel Wine Estate and Restaurant, Plattekloof Road, Panorama, Cape Town, 7500
+27 21 558 6280
www.degrendel.co.za/pages/restaurant
GPS: S33°51'29.42" E18°33'36.63"

De Grendel (meaning 'the latch' in Dutch) farm has been in the Graaff family for four generations. Start your sojourn on this estate in Panorama by taking a moment to see the full benefit of the setting, and then taste the wines. The heritage and history of the Graaff family is evident if you can take your eyes off the typical artist's view of Table Mountain. Blue-and-white plates, family photographs and paintings do little to distract; it is more likely that you will want to watch the chefs at work in the glassed kitchen. Decor, too, is unembellished, allowing the restaurant experience to be all about the food.

Chef Ian Bergh's history lists La Colombe, Kurland, Five Flies and Pure, and he has been with De Grendel since the restaurant opened. He is a locavore, passionate about maximising local produce. Rather than writing on the menu what he will be doing with the ingredients, they are simply listed. The uncomplicated menu alters daily, and is classic yet creative with well-balanced flavour combinations. Your interest will be piqued when seeing brandy and Coke ice cream and liquid popcorn on the menu. Food is created to complement the selection of De Grendel wines, which are offered at cellar door prices.

"The uncomplicated menu alters daily, and is classic yet creative..."

Delaire Graff Restaurant

'sunshine cuisine' – seasonal, local, stylish

Helshoogte Road,
Stellenbosch, 7600
+27 21 885 8160
www.delaire.co.za/dining/the-delaire-graff-restaurant
GPS: S33°55'14.91"
E18°55'08.92"

Delaire Graff is the ultimate in style and sophistication. A stay at the exclusive lodges with private pools and enviable views gives a discerning traveller time to breathe in a tranquil sanctuary offering world-class wines and art, a stunning spa, luxury boutiques and breathtaking landscapes.

At the Delaire Graff Restaurant one can appreciate the interior style or eat on the terrace and take advantage of the panoramic vista of the Stellenbosch valley and vineyards. South African chef Michael Deg creates contemporary menus based on his 'green gastronomy'. Produce is seasonal and sustainable, sourced largely from the on-site greenhouse and vegetable gardens.

'The seasons guide me in creating each dish and a beautiful menu. My love of tomatoes means I will always have a few dishes based around them during summer. In winter I won't even have them in my kitchen because they are not in season. My favourite time of year is spring, when we have fresh peas, broad beans, artichokes and baby fennel, all in our estate garden. Having wonderful seasonal produce locally and on the estate means a never-ending source of inspiration.' Michael loves cooking vegetables. 'The possibilities are endless. In winter, my favourite is cauliflower, and at home during summer, there is nothing better than eating a big bowl of steamed local white asparagus with some simple hollandaise and a glass of sauvignon blanc.' His favourite dish is their goat's cheese appetiser.

They support farmers who produce free-range and pasture-fed livestock. 'Sustainability is central to our philosophy. I try to have a good relationship with my local suppliers to ensure that we are being responsible with that which we put on a plate. We can appreciate the ingredient and where they come from, and ultimately the food will taste better because great food begins with the best ingredients.'

Every Friday a few dishes on the menu change to keep it fresh and to allow it to evolve with the seasons. 'We discuss the changes as a kitchen team and everyone can express their ideas. I find this encourages passion and creativity within the young chefs, and between us we come up with something special that we all enjoy cooking.' Michael earmarks Terroir and The Restaurant at Waterkloof for special occasions; for casual eating he enjoys exploring Bree Street, especially Chefs Warehouse & Canteen.

Michael Deg's goat's cheese croquettes

INGREDIENTS

Goat's cheese croquettes

4 eggs
200g good quality goat's cheese, sliced into 50g portions
100g cake flour
200g panko crumbs

Beetroot purée

3kg large beetroot
200ml cream
100g butter
salt

Beetroot mousse

200ml cream
4 gelatine leaves
500ml beetroot purée

Pickled apple

100ml brown sugar
200ml white wine vinegar
300ml white wine
sprig thyme
1 star anise
2 Granny Smith apples

Candied walnuts

100g castor sugar
100ml water
100g walnuts

Blowtorched goat's cheese

200g good quality goat's cheese, sliced into 50g portions

METHOD

Goat's cheese croquettes

Make an egg wash with the eggs and a little water. Roll the goat's cheese portions in the flour, then the egg wash, then the crumbs, then back into the egg wash and back into the crumbs (it is important to do this twice to prevent them from breaking up in the fryer). Once crumbed, keep in the fridge until needed.

Beetroot purée

Roast the beetroot whole in the oven at 180°C until a small knife can go through easily (approximately 90 minutes). Let them cool. Using your hands, peel off the skin, then chop up the beetroot and transfer to a blender. Add the cream, butter and a pinch of salt and blend until really smooth.

Beetroot mousse

Whip the cream until soft peaks form. Slake the gelatine in cold water until soft. Warm 100ml of the purée and whisk in the gelatine until smooth. Do not boil. Add this to the remaining purée and allow to set in a tray in the fridge for three hours.

Pickled apple

Place everything but the apples in a saucepan and bring to the boil to make the pickling liquid. Remove from heat once boiled and allow to cool until lukewarm. Using a melon baller, scoop balls out of the apples and place them in the pickling liquid. Wrap them tightly so that they don't oxidise, and keep them in the fridge for 24 hours.

Candied walnuts

Bring the sugar and water to the boil, then add the walnuts and boil for two minutes. Strain, then bake the walnuts in the oven at 150°C for 20 minutes until golden brown.

Blowtorched goat's cheese

Scorch the goat's cheese portions with a blowtorch.

TO ASSEMBLE

Fry the croquettes until golden brown. Quenelle the mousse. Make a design of your choice on the plate with the purée, and place all the components neatly on the plate. Garnish with edible flowers and beetroot shavings, serve with a glass of sauvignon blanc and enjoy!
Serves 4

"...ultimately the food will taste better because great food begins with the best ingredients."

CHEF MICHAEL DEG

Don Armando

robust Argentinean grills

20 Cobern Street,
Green Point, Cape Town, 8005
+27 21 418 1462
www.mastrantonio.com/
don-armando
GPS: S33°54'51.83"
E18°25'07.53"

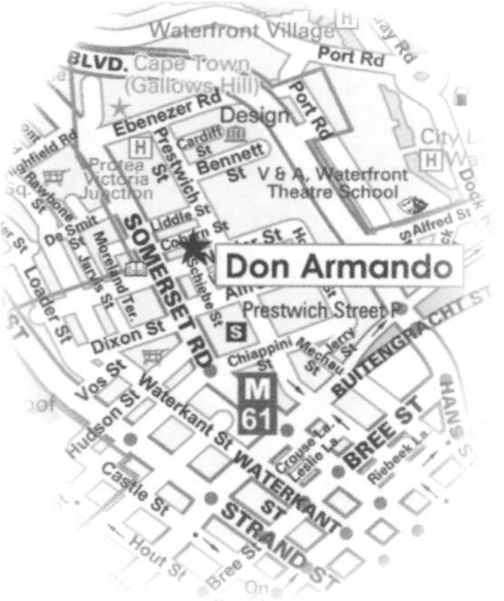

Tucked away in Cobern Street in trendy Green Point, surrounded by many other 'go-to' eating spots, is this macho-feel yet stylish Argentinian steak-house. It will undoubtedly give the old stalwarts a great run for their money in terms of competition.

If a great steak is what you are looking for then you will be more than satisfied here. This hot spot is frequented by couples (who are likely to share the 800g picanha), groups and manly carnivores. They focus on char-grilled meat ('asado'), with their 'grillados' taking centre stage. Choose from the ubiquitous cuts of fillet, sirloin, T-bone and short rib, or pork and lamb chops, but be surprised with the delightful tangy addition of chimichurri with your order. Even the chicken is elevated by this addition. Vegetarians can order a selection of starters such as the grilled provolone with sun-dried tomatoes or the vegetarian empanadas. The prawn skewers served with grilled fennel are superb, as is the quinoa and grilled vegetables. The generous and interesting array of 'guarniciones' (sides), like the white or green bean salad and sweet potato chips, also adds variety to the menu and does more than merely fill the gaps.

Service is warm and friendly, and the chef patron, Daniel Toledo, who named the restaurant after his father, is likely to be in attendance. Argentinian wines feature on the small wine list. Be brave and order something interesting, like the blood sausage or sweetbreads from the 'entratas' section, or something generous like a 500g T-bone steak. Go big or go home?

dw eleven-13

explore the unknown

Dunkeld West Shopping Centre,
Corner Jan Smuts and Bompas
streets, Dunkeld West, 2196
+27 11 325 2843
www.dw11-13.co.za
GPS: S26°07'52.37"
E28°02'05.66"

Named after its location, this gem of superlative experimental gastronomy is neatly tucked away in a quiet and uninspiring shopping centre in Dunkeld West. Sophisticated yet soothing decor is welcoming, playing second fiddle to the flavourful and exquisitely presented food. Lunchtimes are filled with lively conversation; by night it is more intimate and really special. The wine list has been carefully compiled and is, like the menu, aimed at the discerning palate. Creative genius Marthinus Ferreira, with his mischievous smile, and his team do everything to ensure that guests feel at home and are enamoured by the unforgettable food. It is a family affair - his mother and sister are part of the squad. Go for the degustation menu or take some time to choose from the à la carte. Mention that you do not want to have alcohol and you will instead savour a non-alcoholic pairing with each course. His polenta, cauliflower espuma with sultanas, pine nuts, kale and brown butter is the stuff that dreams are made of. Try, too, his Brie ice cream with poached pear, pepper crumble, rocket and port gel. Presentation is truly exquisite and each course is crafted on something interesting, be it a plate or slate. Little touches, like his cutlery laid down French-style, show intimate care with detail.

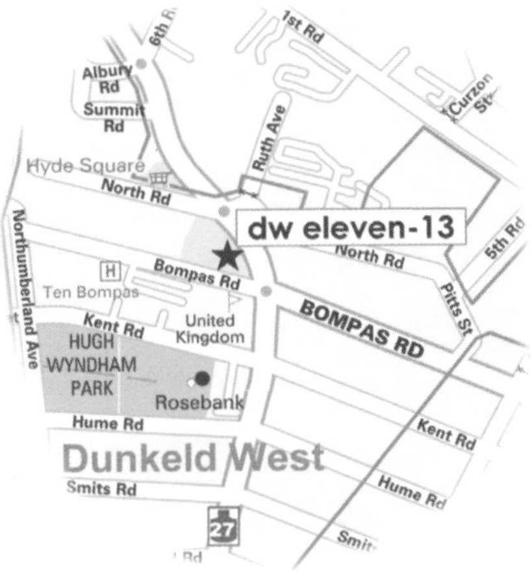

You will ooh and aah after a few hours of appreciating every nuance of his meal, leaving on a high note. Fly there, drive there, but get there. For more of Marthinus's talent on a casual note, go to the Grazing Room next door where the tapas selection will keep your taste buds hopping.

For good food cooked by other great chefs, Marthinus goes to the Foodbarn (he raves about their tripe), Jordan's, Chefs Warehouse & Canteen and Overture in the Cape, and to The Leopard and Local Grill locally.

INGREDIENTS

Salmon
500g salmon
coarse salt

Cucumber ketchup
250ml cucumber juice
62.5ml white wine vinegar
87.5g sugar
25g gellan

Pickled cucumber
200ml water
200ml sugar
200ml white wine vinegar
100g brunoise cucumber

Oyster coulis
28ml milk
3 oysters
½ tablespoon Dijon mustard
100ml vegetable oil
salt and pepper

Grilled cucumber hearts
1 whole cucumber

Shallot vinaigrette
½ shallot
100ml champagne vinegar

Salmon dressing
10ml sherry vinegar
30ml olive oil

Fish skin
reserved salmon skin

Garnish
chopped fresh dill
salmon roe
Granny Smith apple slices
sunflower shoots

METHOD
Salmon
Cure salmon in coarse salt for two hours. Wash off the salt and remove the bones and skin from the fish. Reserve the skin. Cut salmon into portions and sear in a frying pan. Leave to cool. Using clingwrap, roll the salmon and freeze.

Cucumber ketchup
Boil 125ml of the cucumber juice with the white wine vinegar and sugar. Hand blend and gradually add the gellan. Cool in the fridge until set. Using a food processor, blitz the set jelly and add the remaining cucumber juice.

Pickled cucumber
Make pickling liquid by combining the water, sugar and vinegar. Add the cucumber to the liquid and leave for 20 minutes.

Oyster coulis
Blitz the milk, oysters and Dijon mustard in a food processor. Gradually add the oil. Add salt and pepper to taste.

Grilled cucumber hearts
Divide the cucumber into three (lengthways). Remove the sides of the cucumber, leaving the heart. Tightly vac pack it, and leave in the fridge for a day. Grill the cucumber hearts.

Shallot vinaigrette
Finely chop the shallot, then add the vinegar.

Salmon dressing
Combine the vinegar and the oil and mix well.

Fish skin
Remove scales and any remaining flesh from the skin. Place the skin on a flat tray lined with greaseproof paper. Place another flat tray on top to flatten the skin. Place in the oven and heat at 160°C until the skin is dry.

PLATING
Smear a little cucumber ketchup on a plate to form a base. Scatter dill and pickled cucumber on the cucumber ketchup base. Cut cucumber into a rectangle and cut asymmetrically into two halves, placing a half each on opposite sides of the ketchup base. Place salmon rounds on the ketchup base. Add dollops of oyster coulis on the base. Add shallot vinaigrette and salmon roe on the salmon rounds. Thinly slice Granny Smith apples into half-moons and place on asymmetrical cucumbers. Crack three pieces of fish skin; use one piece to lean directly on the cucumber heart and secure the rest on the oyster dollops. Finish off by lightly dressing the dish with the salmon dressing. Garnish with sunflower shoots.

Salmon sashimi

"Presentation is truly exquisite and each course is crafted on something interesting, be it a plate or slate."

Eat

modern yet accessible cuisine

'L Corro Shopping Centre, Corner 14th Avenue and Bagley Terrace, Northcliff, 2195
+27 11 476 3749
GPS: S26°08'41.03"
E27°57'15.16"

The setting is every restaurateur's dream - a simple indoor space with an outside courtyard in a quiet suburban shopping centre in Northcliff. Add white tablecloths and a muted colour palette of earthy tones with a splash of colourful artwork, and you have a popular eatery.

Classically trained Philippe Wagenführer has breathed new life into this once ailing local bistro. By making a few tweaks to enhance the light and airy decor, he's turned the venue into what he fondly refers to as a fine dining, community restaurant. Rather than designing a menu for the public, he has earned respect from regulars by offering them exactly what they want - good value, quality dishes and outstanding service. He's moved away from dabbling in molecular food and now he uses the whole plate to create 'landscapes'. On the tasting menu is a landscape of smoked chicken with spicy watermelon and pineapple, served with a Thai dressing. It's a dish that grows on you with each mouthful and has your taste buds cheering for more.

"It's a dish that grows on you with each mouthful and has your taste buds cheering for more."

The menu changes with the seasons, but the very well-priced four-course tasting menu is a sensory introduction to his kitchen's prowess. All the elements on the plate come together beautifully with layers of flavour and texture. Presentation is simple yet impressive, and dishes are paired with custom-made wines, especially blended to Philippe's requirements.

'I didn't want my menu to be too elaborate - it's real, home-cooked food with substance. I know the reality of the economy so I want to offer the best value-for-money fine dining in a convivial setting.'

El Burro

innovative and authentic Mexican

81 Main Road, Green Point,
Cape Town, 8005
+27 21 433 2364
www.elburro.co.za
GPS: S33°54'30.76"
E18°24'39.23"

Vivacious and traditionally dressed waitresses offer a warm welcome as you climb the stairs to El Burro. Situated on the Green Point 'strip', as it is termed, it gives a grandstand view of Cape Town Stadium, with indoor tables too. There is nothing downmarket about their grub or decor, and the vibe feels fabulous. It has a homely atmosphere, and before long conversation hides any traditional background music.

The best tip for too much chilli is to touch the end of your tongue with salt, but at El Burro patrons are seen to avoid good advice and enjoy the craft beers and tequila instead. Try their ceviche or chilli rellenos to start. The Carne Asada – free-range rib-eye steak served on crushed new potatoes with sour cream, roast garlic, pickled jalapeños and tomato salsa – is a must. The linefish marinated in ginger with chilli and preserved lemon and the enchiladas rojo are flavour-filled and very memorable. Vegetarians have good options, with the aubergine, artichoke and spinach quesadilla being a standout.

Ellerman House

honest and fresh, forever creative

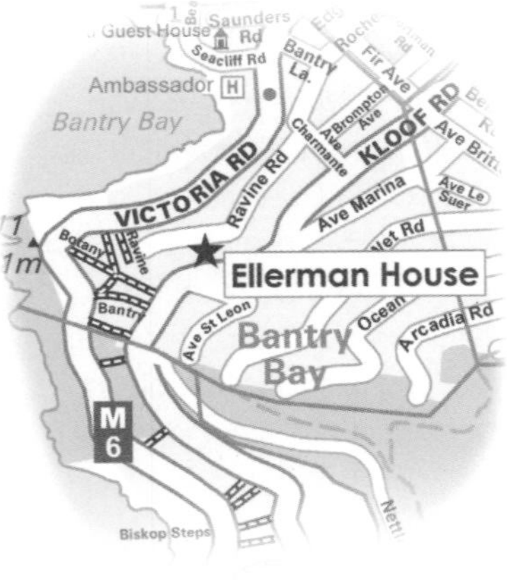

The only way to sample Veronica Canha-Hibbert's ever-evolving cuisine is to treat yourself to an overnight stay. Once the stately home of Sir John and Lady Ellerman, distinguished shipping magnates and investors, Ellerman House, on the slopes of Lion's Head in prestigious Bantry Bay, is now privately owned. This elegant Cape Edwardian mansion stands as an icon of South Africa's finest cuisine, private art collection and breathtaking wine cellar, art in itself. The privacy afforded by not being open to the public offers mystique for locals and luxury for guests, and the two sumptuous villas are often a home from home for visiting celebrities.

Executive chef Veronica is of Portuguese origin, born in Wellington and was inspired to cook from a young age thanks to her mother's wonderful feats in the kitchen. Her favourite ingredients are garlic, lemons, bay leaves and beetroot, especially the heirloom varieties of different colours. She loves curries and showcasing the Bo-Kaap influence to guests.

"...its cuisine is in a modern European style using quality local ingredients."

Crediting the hospitality industry with allowing her to see the world and meet fascinating people, Veronica trained at the Mount Nelson under legendary chef Garth Stroebel (where she met husband Craig, executive pastry chef) and joined Ellerman House in 2008. The 11-bedroom boutique hotel caters mostly to an international clientele of American, European and British guests, and as a result its cuisine is in a modern European style using quality local ingredients. Daily text messages from suppliers inspire Veronica to plan each daily lunch and dinner menu, a challenging feat that she relishes with aplomb. The superior menus are expertly matched with wines selected by Chilean sommelier Manny Cabello from their jaw-droppingly impressive wine cellar. This Relais & Châteaux property is true destination dining.

180 Kloof Road,
Bantry Bay, Cape Town, 8005
+27 21 430 3200
www.ellerman.co.za/experience/cuisine
GPS: S33°55'44.75" E18°22'39.88"

INGREDIENTS

Pork belly

canola oil
1.2kg pork belly, cut into 200g pieces
1 litre white wine
1 litre water
1 teaspoon paprika
1 teaspoon garam masala
1 teaspoon saffron threads
1 teaspoon ground ginger
1 teaspoon ground cumin
1 tablespoon veal stock
3 cloves garlic, chopped
2 tablespoons light brown sugar

Tahini carrot purée

Maldon salt to taste
500g carrots, peeled and halved crossways
2 tablespoons butter
1/2 cup tahini
juice and zest of 1 lemon
1 tablespoon chopped ginger
2 cloves garlic
salt and pepper to taste
1 teaspoon ground cumin
2 tablespoons extra virgin olive oil

Sesame Vichy carrots

500g baby carrots, trimmed and peeled (retain the green tips)
Maldon salt to taste
2 tablespoons sherry vinegar
2 tablespoons honey
2 tablespoons extra virgin olive oil
1/2 teaspoon finely chopped fresh thyme leaves
1/2 teaspoon white sesame seeds
1 tablespoon cold unsalted butter
salt and black pepper to taste

Pak choy

2 tablespoons peanut oil
2 cloves garlic, peeled and minced
3 tablespoons peeled, minced ginger
4 bunches (500g) baby pak choy
1 tablespoon soy sauce
1 tablespoon chicken stock
toasted sesame seed oil for drizzling

Garnish

micro coriander

METHOD

Pork belly

Preheat oven to 180°C. Heat a heavy-based saucepan (which has a tight-fitting lid) over medium heat. Once hot, drizzle in a bit of canola oil and brown all the sides of the pork belly pieces. Once all the pieces are browned, remove from the saucepan and deglaze with the white wine. Pour a litre of water into the saucepan and add all the spices, the veal stock, the chopped garlic and the sugar. Stir to dissolve and bring to the boil. Once a rolling boil has been achieved, remove from the heat. Return the pork belly to the saucepan and ensure that the meat is submerged in liquid. Cover the saucepan with the lid and place in the oven. Confit the pork for two hours, turning frequently. Cook until the pork is tender and the liquid has evaporated. Remove from the oven and allow to cool slightly in the saucepan. Retain the pan juices to serve as an aromatic jus.

Tahini carrot purée

Bring a medium-sized saucepan of water to a boil and season with Maldon salt. Add carrots and butter and cook until tender, about 10 minutes. Drain and transfer the carrots to a blender along with the tahini, lemon juice and zest, ginger and garlic. Season with salt, pepper and cumin. Purée until smooth and add the olive oil to the purée while the motor is running.

Sesame Vichy carrots

Put carrots in a sauté pan, season with Maldon salt and add one tablespoon of the sherry vinegar. Add cold water until the carrots are half submerged. Set pan over high heat and bring liquid to a boil. Turn heat down to medium and cook, stirring occasionally, until carrots are just cooked through – about 15 minutes. Once carrots are cooked through, discard any excess liquid in the pan. Add the remaining tablespoon of sherry vinegar to the pan, along with the honey, olive oil, thyme, white sesame seeds and cold butter. Cook for about two minutes to glaze the carrots. Season to taste with salt and pepper. Serve immediately.

Pak choy

In a large sauté pan with a lid, heat the peanut oil over medium-high heat until it starts to simmer. Add garlic and ginger and cook, stirring constantly, until fragrant – about 45 seconds. Add pak choy and stir carefully to cover with peanut oil, then cook for approximately two minutes. Add soy sauce and stock, then cover the pan and cook for approximately two minutes more, until steam begins to escape from beneath the lid of the pan. Uncover and continue to cook until liquid is close to evaporated and stalks are soft to the touch – approximately three minutes. Toss with toasted sesame seed oil before serving.

PLATING

Use a hot main course plate. Just off-centre, dollop a large tablespoon of tahini carrot purée and spread to a taper. Place a neatly folded pak choy on the plate. Place the pork belly diagonally over the pak choy. Scatter approximately 100g of sesame Vichy carrots around the plate. Drizzle with aromatic jus. Garnish with micro coriander.
Serves 6

Confit pork belly with tahini carrot purée, sesame Vichy carrots, baby pak choy and aromatic jus

Erawan

a perfect balance of flavours

On the popular eatery street, Wolfe Street in Chelsea Village, Wynberg, sits the original Erawan restaurant. It set the bar for Thai in the town. Following the success of this authentic Thai restaurant, which has an understated elegance about it, they doubled their popularity in Johannesburg.

Authentic Thai tastes are married with warm and friendly Asian hospitality. Chef Noom Withum finds his inspiration from his home country, Thailand, and meets the challenge of using local ingredients to recreate authentic Thai food. He is constantly inspired by the fresh ingredients that South Africa has to offer, but cannot help making seafood a definite favourite. His premium dish is the Par Nueng Sam Rod – steamed fish on a bed of fresh vegetables served with a choice of oyster, curry or Thai spicy sauce.

'Thai cuisine is a perfect balance of flavours. With every mouthful you must taste exactly enough salty, sour and sweet flavours. Ingredients like chilli, lemongrass, fish sauce and coconut milk are the type of ingredients that are very pronounced in Thai cuisine. Seasonal produce is very important too, as in Thai cooking we need the most flavour we can extract from ingredients. Our Johannesburg restaurant has Som Tam on the menu, using green papaya, but as its seasonal period is so short in Cape Town, we have adjusted the recipe to contain carrots. We only use meat from sustainable local butcheries and, because of my love for seafood, we only order from reputable suppliers.'

There are no surprises at Erawan – to ensure consistency, the menu does not change often, but they do add and change a few dishes for interest.

'To be very honest, my favourite meal is with my Thai colleagues, friends and family. We eat together every evening and this is definitely my most favourite as it reminds me of home and where I came from.'

15 Wolfe Street, Wynberg,
Cape Town, 7800
+27 21 797 5000
www.erawan.co.za
GPS: S34°00'25.07"
E18°27'47.26"

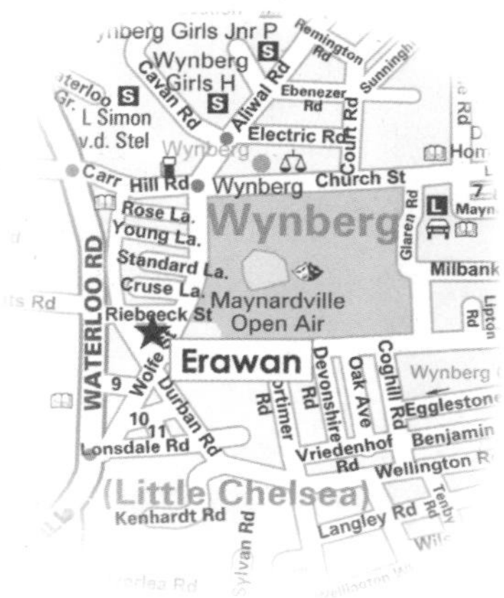

INGREDIENTS

½ Thai duck per portion
broth
selection of soy sauces
oyster sauce
¼ white onion, chopped
½ leek, shredded
½ green pepper, chopped
½ red pepper, chopped
5 mushrooms, diced
½ carrot, chopped
5 florets broccoli
5 florets cauliflower
handful shredded cabbage
4 green beans
garlic to taste
ginger to taste
1 large spoonful of Erawan's signature stir-fry sauce

METHOD

Simmer the Thai ducks in broth with the soy sauces and oyster sauce. Gently debone the duck and set aside for frying. In a hot wok, stir-fry the vegetables, garlic and ginger with the stir-fry sauce.

Simultaneously shallow-fry the duck until crispy. To serve, top the vegetables with the duck, and finish off with some small cut carrots, green beans in a special glaze, and coriander. Serve with steamed jasmine rice or egg noodles.

Erawan's signature crispy duck

Foliage

back to the future, back to nature

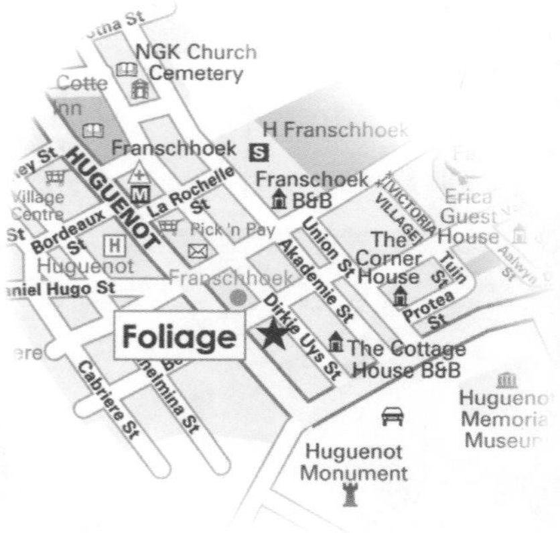

11 Huguenot Road,
Franschhoek, 7690
+27 21 876 2328
www.foliage.co.za
GPS: S33°54'45.95"
E19°07'17.48"

In the main street of the Cape's culinary capital, Franschhoek, is a discreet door. Behind it, a new way of sourcing and serving food is unfolding. An adventure awaits. There is breathtaking art on the walls from neighbouring Is Art Gallery. Expect quirky sculptures, expect quirky food, and meet the quirky chef who made headlines at La Motte. Now Chris is doing it his way.

Chris Erasmus serves a cuisine that should be called a philosophy. He believes in and demonstrates the ethos of truly living off the land, reducing the carbon footprint. His menu changes daily, depending on what has been foraged. They forage twice a day – the boys do the rough stuff, the girls pick the pretties, and mushrooms, which are dangerous, they all do together. Proof of his dedication is seen in well-worn Wellington boots and a bucket or two in the restaurant. They make cheese. They ferment beer. The rest of the proof is on the plate. Plates are mostly of natural materials, like wood. The wooden butter knives are whittled by one of his chefs in his free time. You can work your way through the small, interesting menu or, for a casual lunch, simply share some starters – the spiced zebra dumplings, the charcoal-roasted beetroot salad, the Tom Yum broth or the goose liver. Try the chocolate pot plant for the ultimate in desserts.

Nothing is ever the same. You may even have roadkill – a friend drove over a porcupine by mistake, so brought it to Chris to cook it respectfully. Here the customer comes second, the produce first; in his words, 'The farmers are the rock stars.' He sees his restaurant as a lifestyle, not a money-making machine, and believes that chefs should stay in their kitchens rather than be distracted by copious commercial opportunities.

Chris likes to eat at Burrata and Bocca, Bread & Wine, and at Jordan's. His colleagues and competitors are friends. His open kitchen allows guests and friends to witness passion at work. There is no front of house and behind the scenes. There is a feeling of the earth and being grounded there – authenticity at its best.

"We are going backwards, using ingredients that are available here..."

CHEF CHRIS ERASMUS

He truly takes one back to nature. Here is a special man in a special place, doing more than special things with his ingredients. In his words, 'We are going backwards, using ingredients that are available here, and even bartering.' Let's all go backwards.

Valrhona chocolate pot plant with carrot mascarpone, rose chocolate rocks and buchu ice cream

INGREDIENTS

Chocolate pot plant, pastry

250g cake flour
125g pecan nuts
20g porcini powder
1 egg
150g soft butter

Chocolate pot plant, filling

400g Valrhona Guanaja 70% dark chocolate
100g milk
300g cream
2 eggs

Carrot mascarpone

1kg carrots
1 cup good quality full-fat mascarpone

Rose chocolate rocks

220g Valrhona Guanaja 70% dark chocolate
1/2 teaspoon rose water
30g butter
125g cream
1/2 cup cocoa powder for dusting

Buchu ice cream

500g cream
500g milk
10g dried buchu
160g egg yolks
180g castor sugar

Garnish

wood sorrel
edible flowers such as dandelions, pansies, rocket, mustard

METHOD

Chocolate pot plant, pastry

Place the flour and nuts in a food processor and blend until fine.
Add the remaining ingredients and pulse until incorporated. Wrap the pastry and refrigerate for two hours before use. Lightly butter 100ml dariole moulds and press the pastry onto the inner sides and base of the moulds, about 3mm thick. Refrigerate for 15 minutes, line with tinfoil and fill with rice or any dried pulses. Bake for 12 minutes at 170°C, remove the tinfoil and bake for a further four minutes until the pastry is dry to the touch and cooked. Place 100g of the pastry in a bowl, sprinkle with a teaspoon of cocoa powder and bake until crispy; this will be used as a soil.

Chocolate pot plant, filling

Preheat the oven to 105°C. Place the chocolate in a bowl. Bring the milk and cream to a boil and pour over the chocolate. Stir until smooth, add the eggs and stir again until smooth. Pour the mix into the pot plant cases and bake for 12–15 minutes until just set. Leave to cool slightly and serve at ambient temperature.

Carrot mascarpone

Peel the carrots and juice them. Pour the juice through a muslin cloth and pour into a saucepan. Cook until syrupy and add to the cheese. Whisk to incorporate. Refrigerate.

Rose chocolate rocks

Place the chocolate, rose water and butter into a bowl and place over a saucepan with boiling water. Stir until melted. Bring the cream to a boil in a saucepan and pour over the chocolate; stir until incorporated. Place the bowl over ice and whisk until the mix starts to set and become lighter. Place in a piping bag and pipe rock shapes onto a tray lined with greaseproof paper. Place in the freezer for 20 minutes and toss in the cocoa powder. Refrigerate until needed.

Buchu ice cream

Place the cream, milk and buchu in a saucepan and bring to a boil. Place the egg yolks and sugar in a bowl and whisk until fluffy. Pour the milk mixture through a fine sieve and add half the mixture to the eggs. Whisk well and pour the mix back into the milk in the saucepan. Cook over low heat, stirring continuously, until the mix reaches 68°C or it coats the back of a wooden spoon. Pour through a sieve into a bowl over ice and stir until cold. Churn in an ice-cream churner until set. You can churn it by hand by placing the bowl in the freezer and whisking it every 10 minutes until set.

Gabriëlskloof

honest, hearty fare with flair

Deep in the heart of the Overberg, outside Botrivier, lies the family-owned and run Gabriëlskloof Wine Estate. Established in 2000, here guests from far and wide come to sample their wines, their olives and to enjoy a relaxed meal in the stylish yet understated restaurant. Their deli is as tempting – filled to the brim with their wines, hand-picked olives and cold-pressed olive oils, and appetising artisanal produce.

Frans Groenewald grew up in a family with a catering business and was always involved in this with his parents, and since then has added to his culinary inspiration through travelling, reading and dining out. 'I prefer to work with fresh herbs, fresh fish and local produce to create my style of cooking – South African-inspired bistro-style food. I love a good Beef Wellington. As far as possible, I support sustainability and source from suppliers with the same approach. My menu changes by the season, which makes it easy to cook with produce that is in season.'

Produce is sourced from neighbouring farms. There is a no-fuss feel to his hearty and wholesome fare, and the ambience, although elegant, is relaxed and welcoming. Not surprising, as Frans and Mariaan are passionate about the estate and all that it offers. Food is simply presented and perfectly complemented by the estate wines. 'I love dining in fine dining restaurants like The Test Kitchen, and for a casual meal, nothing beats a braai with my family and friends.'

R43, Botrivier, 7185
+27 28 284 9865
www.gabrielskloof.co.za/restaurant
GPS: S34°14'19.88" E19°15'09.69"

INGREDIENTS

300ml Gabriëlskloof olive oil
1kg rainbow trout, pin boned
250g exotic mushrooms
50ml soy sauce
juice of 2 lemons
50g fresh coriander
25ml sherry vinegar

METHOD

Warm the olive oil to 60°C and poach the trout in it for six to eight minutes, depending on the thickness. Fry the mushrooms. Combine the soy sauce, lemon juice, coriander and vinegar to form the dressing, and add the mushrooms. Now also add 100ml of the poaching liquid to the dressing.

TO SERVE

Place trout on top of either a salad or warm sweet potatoes, and spoon the warm dressing over the fish.

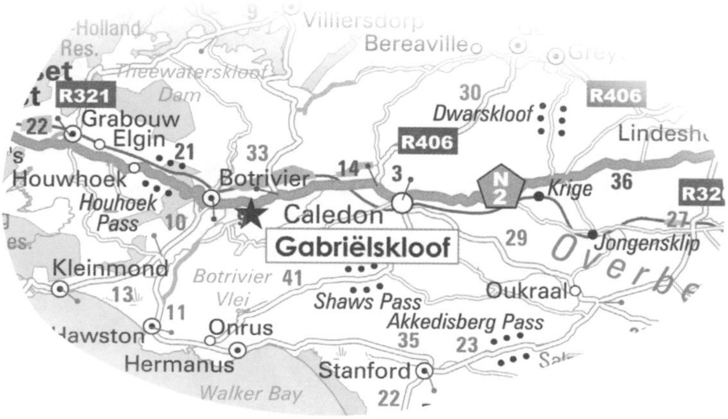

Olive oil-poached trout with exotic mushrooms

Grande Provence

imaginative and innovative fine dining

History and heritage are visible. So are flavour and passion. Here Darren Badenhorst, chef at Grande Provence Heritage Wine Estate in Franschhoek, chooses ingredients according to seasonality, variety and availability, and for him consistency is key.

Main Road,
Franschhoek, 7690
+27 21 876 8600
www.grandeprovence.co.za/cuisine/the-restaurant
GPS: S33°54'05.88"
E19°06'27.19"

'Local, fresh, interesting and organic ingredients are at the top of my list. All ingredients have the potential to be something interesting. That being said, I am enjoying mushrooms at the moment ... the different textures, depth of flavours and the sheer variety on offer is a chef's dream.' He describes his cuisine as classic French building blocks with an Asian influence.

His playfulness and imagination are evident on the plate. 'I draw inspiration from many different channels of day-to-day life and my past. The Cape Winelands have so much to offer and I try to utilise everything, governed by the seasons. My food is a direct reflection of the mood I was in when I created it. Food is seen before it is eaten, so I try to capture each ingredient as artistically as I can. I want to create a memorable experience for diners, from when the plate arrives to the conversations they have after the meal.'

Darren loves to eat at home, believing that food is best enjoyed with the right company and some of the finest wines in the country that are available on his doorstep. The days of eating out to fill your stomach are a thing of the past. Dining out is an experience to be appreciated and savoured, shared with good friends and paired with great wine. 'If you can't remember the details of the meal you had last night, what's the point?' says Badenhorst.

INGREDIENTS

Rabbit

6 rabbits
1 x 500g block butter, clarified and beurre noisette
60ml mustard seeds for the butter paint
transglutimate

Rabbit farce

2 boneless chicken breasts
400g bacon
zest of 5 lemons
1 bunch thyme
salt and pepper to taste
transglutimate to bind lightly
Wagyu fat
1-1.5 litres cream
3 whole eggs and 3 egg whites
smoke essence to taste

Rabbit liver and foie gras parfait

1 medium onion
5-7 cloves garlic
6 tronchons (slices) foie gras
60ml allspice
4 whole cloves
25ml Szechuan pepper, whole
250g rabbit livers
750g duck livers
1 bunch thyme
120ml sherry
120ml local port
1 ½ x 500g blocks butter (to make 1 cup beurre noisette - check if more is needed)
4 eggs
1-1 ½ cups cream
black pepper and fossil salt

Mustard pomme purée

10 whole potatoes
1.5 litres cream
½ x 500g block butter
salt to taste
2 sprigs thyme
5 black peppercorns
wholegrain mustard

Pumpkin seed gremolata

pumpkin seeds
lemon zest
yuzu zest
finely chopped parsley
olive oil
Maldon salt

Parsnip crisps

5 medium parsnips
oil for deep-frying

Garnish

deep-fried pancetta crisps
courgettes
jus
micro herbs and baby leaves

METHOD

Rabbit

Clean and debone rabbits and bring to room temperature. Trim off excess meat and keep livers aside. Paint clingwrap with plain butter then season to taste. Place rabbits head to toe on the clingwrap, then paint with mustard butter and season accordingly. Dust lightly with transglutimate. Pipe in the farce, then wrap tightly. Vac pack and cook at 63.5°C for four hours - refresh for one hour.

Rabbit farce

Cold smoke the chicken breasts, then mix all the ingredients for the farce in a food processor and check seasoning. Place in a piping bag.

Rabbit liver and foie gras parfait

Sweat off onion and garlic in the foie gras with spices until all the fat is rendered and spices are cooked. Add the livers and thyme and cook off lightly, then use the sherry and port to deglaze fully. Blend in a food processor with the beurre noisette, eggs and cream, and season to taste. Strain through a drum sieve and check seasoning again. Cook off in a tray lined with wax paper. Cook for 35-45 minutes at 140°C in a water bath, covered with tinfoil. Let rest in the fridge for at least two to three hours.

Mustard pomme purée

Peel the potatoes and cook in seasoned cream and butter mix with the thyme, to infuse, and the black peppercorns. Strain off the cream mix and reserve. Pass the potatoes through a drum sieve. Incorporate the reserved cream back into the potato mix, then sieve again. Add wholegrain mustard then put into squeeze bottles for plating.

Pumpkin seed gremolata

Toast off pumpkin seeds lightly, zest lemon with a small amount of yuzu zest, add finely chopped parsley and a dash of olive oil and season to taste with Maldon salt. Mix and set aside.

Parsnip crisps

Peel parsnips and slice diagonally so that a tapered wisp is achieved. Fry in clean oil until crisp.

Garnish

Lay out pancetta and flatten, then dust with transglutimate and roll tightly. Rest for at least three hours in fridge. Turn the courgettes. Heat up jus and check consistency. Cut micros and baby leaves, refresh and set aside until required.

"I want to create a memorable experience for diners, from when the plate arrives to the conversations they have after the meal."

CHEF DARREN BADENHORST

Stuffed and rolled rabbit ballotine

The Great Eastern Food Bar

street food on a plate

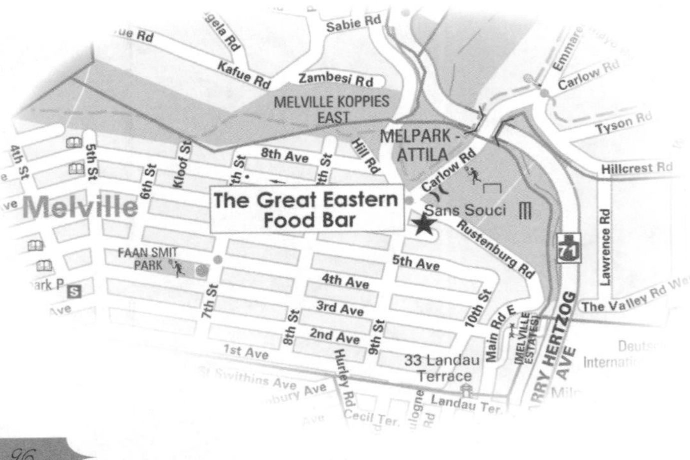

"My menu is world-inspired, with fresh Asian flavours."

CHEF CAROLINA RASENTI

53 Rustenburg Road,
Melville,
Johannesburg, 2092
+27 11 482 2910
GPS: S26°10'28.28"
E28°00'48.93"

This is a destination eatery and no doubt patrons will travel far and wide to Melville to try fresh, adventurous flavours dished up by owner and self-taught cook Carolina Rasenti.

Don't expect authentic dishes made to exact proportions. It's 'globally inspired' cuisine. Carolina interprets Asian food based on research and what she enjoys. Dishes have been designed to be shared, so it's rude not to dip into your partner's plate! A highlight is Carolina's home-made pickles, made from cucumber, ginger, bamboo and even pears, and these textures paired with a noodle dish are sublime. It's vegetarian heaven, with just enough chicken and fish on the menu to keep carnivores satisfied. The spicy Korean fried chicken is a sure thing.

Carolina uses her South American heritage to introduce a special depth of flavour and spiciness to the menu, and she's used her interior design training to create a space that is hip yet functional. One can enjoy views of the north of Jo'burg from the balcony seating.

Service is attentive and portions are generous. Try the sashimi tacos (trout ceviche with pickled lemons and wasabi) and kimchi ginger ramen noodles. For dessert, cinnamon churros made from wonton wrappers with salted caramel dipping sauce is a must. Home-made cordials and drinking vinegars are also a treat, or you can opt for saké, tequila or Asian beer. The wine list is small, featuring boutique wines.

'I wanted a tapas-style dining experience, where people can share food and try new things. It's a great way to eat if you find you can't commit to one dish. My menu is world-inspired, with fresh Asian flavours.'

INGREDIENTS

Ginger pickle

2 cups rice vinegar
1 cup water
2 tablespoons sugar
2 tablespoons salt
1 cup thinly sliced ginger (use a potato peeler)

Wasabi mayo

1/2 tablespoon wasabi powder
1 teaspoon water
3 tablespoons mayonnaise

Taco shells

2 cups flour (your choice)
1/2 teaspoon salt
1/2 cup warm water
cornstarch
canola or palm oil for frying

Trout ceviche/sashimi

250g packet Milly's cold-smoked pieces of trout
1/4 cup ginger pickling liquid
1 tablespoon pure sesame oil

Plating

finely diced lemon pickle
1/4 fresh lime
spring onions
black sesame seeds

METHOD

Ginger pickle

Combine vinegar, water, sugar and salt in a saucepan and bring to the boil. Boil until sugar is dissolved. Remove from the heat and drop ginger slices into the liquid. Allow liquid to cool with the ginger inside. If using in under an hour, jars can sit at room temperature. Otherwise refrigerate for up to a week.

Wasabi mayo

Mix the wasabi powder and the water into a paste, add mayonnaise and stir.

Taco shells

Sift together flour and salt in a bowl. Slowly stir in warm water – the dough will be very stiff. Knead dough on floured surface till smooth, about 15 minutes. Cover with a towel and let stand for 20 minutes. This part takes some elbow grease, so be warned. Roll about a half of the dough out, as thin as you can. It should make 32 x 7cm squares if you're lucky, or sixteen if you're not. Repeat for the other half of the dough. To store, just sprinkle with cornstarch and keep in an airtight bag in the fridge or freezer. Cut the squares into circles. Heat a saucepan with canola or palm oil. Using a pair of tongs, drop a circle into the oil and mould it up against the edge of the saucepan – try to make a boat shape (this will take practice).

Trout Ceviche/Sashimi

Place trout pieces in a large bowl. Spoon the ginger pickling liquid and sesame oil over the trout and mix thoroughly. Let the mixture rest for 15 minutes, covered.

PLATING

Take a fried taco shell, place a small dollop of wasabi mayo on one side, spoon in a tablespoon of trout mix, a small drizzle of sesame oil and the juice of a quarter lime. Place half a teaspoon of diced lemon pickle on the plate, and sprinkle with spring onions and black sesame seeds. Serve with ginger pickle.

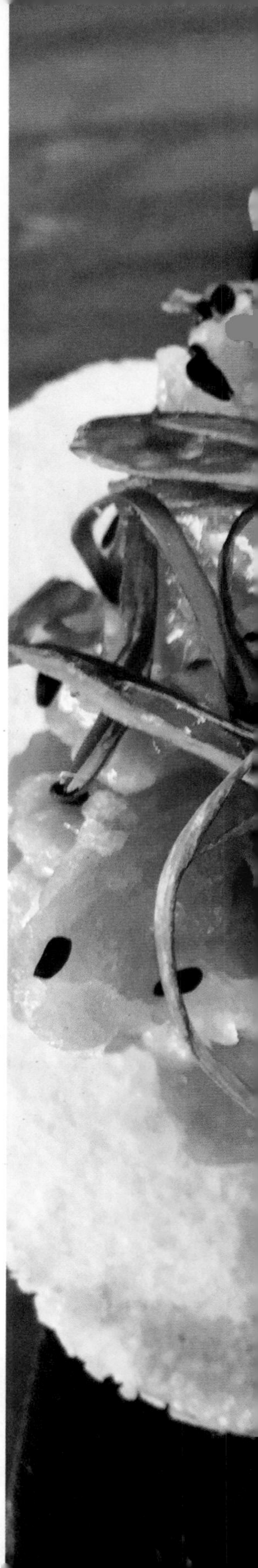

Sashimi tacos (Ceviche tacos)

The Grill Room

carefully considered, never contrived

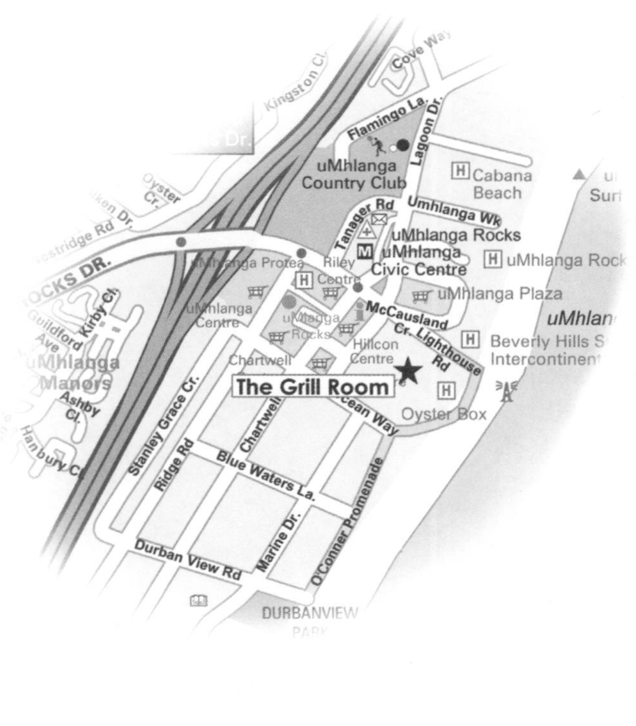

The Oyster Box,
2 Lighthouse Road,
uMhlanga, 4319
+27 31 514 5000
www.oysterboxhotel.com/food-and-drink/the-grill-room
GPS: S29°43'39.22"
E31°05'13.52"

Beautifully positioned in uMhlanga, with sweeping views of the Indian Ocean, the Oyster Box is a landmark hotel anchored by the lighthouse. Part of the international Red Carnation group, its cheerful splashes and stripes of red make it a light and bright, relaxed and happy favourite for travellers. Regulars return for the family-feel five-star service, the setting, the spa and, of course, the food. Visitors to Durban seek its famous curries, and there is no better place to experience top-class curries than at the legendary Ocean Terrace, where no fewer than 11 masterpieces are there to tempt you. The Lighthouse Bar is the perfect place for a special sundowner.

By contrast, the fine dining restaurant, The Grill Room, favours nautical hues of blue and white and an air of formality. Chef Kevin Joseph believes in creating food from scratch, with 95% of foods being prepared on the property (they have their own pastry kitchen), and sourcing from the best local suppliers, whom he terms 'food heroes'. They also have an oyster farm, which pays testament to his ethos of sustainability. 'For every business we support, we are inspiring a community.' He loves seafood and makes a concerted effort to adhere to SASSI guidelines. Core ingredients stay on the menu, the linefish changes daily and the menu evolves seasonally. One favourite dish is his confit of duck. Many, of course, are lured for the oysters, and the grills live up to expectations.

"Core ingredients stay on the menu, the linefish changes daily and the menu evolves seasonally."

The seven-course menu, accompanied by a fine selection of wines, is a real treat and you are sure to hear the odd rendition of 'Happy Birthday' as guests celebrate and make memories. Beauty abounds. Plates are monogrammed William Edwards (the Louis Vuitton of crockery!), the white armchairs soft leather. Every detail is carefully considered and crafted. The starter trolley is an original collector's piece from the Royal Hotel, and the array of dishes showcases the chef's imagination and sense of generosity with great visual appeal. The dessert trolley, an antique, is also breathtaking. There are some real characters at the Oyster Box – Henry Pakiri, the maître d', has been there for well over 50 years, and Scabenga, the cat, is also a long-time favourite. The monkeys come and go.

Whilst Kevin can be found eating at the Green Mango, the Green Parrot, El Firenze or 9th Avenue Bistro, you will find him happiest at home ... he, too, can braai.

INGREDIENTS

Duck

4 duck legs
15g salt per kilogram of duck leg
2–3 sprigs fresh thyme leaves
150g duck fat
150ml extra virgin olive oil
1 shallot, finely sliced
1 clove garlic, finely diced
400g tinned cannellini beans
200g tinned tomatoes, puréed
200ml chicken stock
1 sprig rosemary leaves, finely chopped
salt and pepper
50g salted butter

Celeriac mash

500g floury potatoes, peeled and cut into chunks
500g celeriac, peeled and cut into chunks
75g salted butter
110ml double cream
salt and pepper

METHOD

Duck

Place the duck legs into a roasting tray and sprinkle with salt and thyme. Cover the tray with cling-wrap and chill overnight. Heat a heavy-based frying pan over low to medium heat, place the duck legs in the pan and cover them with duck fat and olive oil. Bring to a gentle simmer and cook the duck legs gently for two hours or until the meat is very tender. Remove the legs from the fat, and place onto a clean roasting tray, draining off and reserving any excess fat. Shred the meat from two of the duck legs. Set the other two aside. Heat a little of the reserved duck fat in a frying pan over a medium heat. Add the shallot and garlic and fry until soft. Add the shredded duck meat, beans, tomatoes, stock and rosemary and return the mixture to the boil. Boil for another two to three minutes, season to taste and whisk in the butter. Heat a little more of the reserved duck fat in a frying pan over high heat. Add the reserved duck legs, skin side down, and fry for two to three minutes, or until the skin is crisp and the duck meat is warmed through.

Celeriac mash

Place the potatoes and celeriac into a saucepan of salted water and bring to the boil. Reduce the heat and simmer for 15 minutes or until tender. Drain well and return to the saucepan to steam over the heat for one minute. Pass the cooked potatoes and celeriac through a ricer until smooth, and then return to the saucepan. Add the butter and cream and mix well before seasoning with salt and pepper to taste.

PLATING

Place some of the mash on each plate, position a duck leg on the mash and spoon over the shredded duck and bean mixture. Serve with a fresh garden salad.

"For every business we support,
we are inspiring a community."

CHEF KEVIN JOSEPH

Confit of duck

The Grillhouse

it's all about the meat

1 The Firs,
Hyatt Centre, Oxford Road
and Biermann Avenue,
Rosebank, Johannesburg, 2196
+27 11 880 3945
www.thegrillhouse.co.za/
grillhouse-rosebank
GPS: S26°08'35.72"
E28°02'33.28"

Even reluctant carnivores appreciate The Grillhouse in Rosebank. Partners Saul Mervis and Joel Katz give guests an animated greeting and roll out the red carpet. Waiters are well trained to answer many questions about the meat and guide you through the expansive menu. You would do well to choose their special of fillet with a wild mushroom sauce or the option of having it covered with their pepper and mustard crust. Try their basting sauce and the penny will drop – know why this restaurant has for 21 years been lauded as the top steakhouse in the town. Meat.inc is also theirs, as is The Grillhouse in Sandton. 'We are meat and potatoes people; that's what we do well,' says Saul.

The restaurant is macho, with private dining areas, leather-studded booths and a warm, welcoming feel. Here they say it is all about the meat – you may say the meat, service, comprehensive wine list and ambience. You may not get gourmet presentation, but they know who they are and what they do well. More importantly, they know what people want. 'We do not offer good service – that you get in a bank. We offer hospitality. We attribute our longevity to consistency.'

Hospitable they are. They also cater for non-carnivores. You will leave with the urgency of returning, or with a bag of biltong purchased from their quality meat outlet at their front door.

Grootbos Private Reserve

making the most of Mother Nature

R43, Gansbaai, 7220
+27 28 384 8053
www.grootbos.com/en/things-to-do/wine-and-dine
GPS: S34°32'30.41" E19°24'12.38"

This slice of unspoilt nature beckons. Close to Hermanus, Gansbaai and Stanford, it is popular with international visitors who come to witness the glory of Walker Bay with its whales and wines. Locals, too, should treat themselves to a sojourn here to understand how an owner can seriously show respect to the land, developing it with conscience. Relax into comfy seats to enjoy the vista before dinner.

A specially conceptualised food and wine pairing will be created for you by their inspired chef, Ben Conradie, and his team. After a decade on the property, he is still ringing the changes, shaping the chefs of the future and using what is growing right there. His menu constantly fluctuates to accommodate what is available, and where possible everything is made from scratch.

'Take one ingredient and pull it apart - see how much you can do with it.' This he does well. His wild mushroom triette provides a good indication of how he likes to take one ingredient and innovate and experiment. Here fresh fish is caught daily in nearby waters - often the same kind of fish, so Ben plays to make sure it is different for guests who are staying for a few days. His love of fresh herbs and spices is evident, as is how he works with the seasons. After an incredible epicurean experience you may wish to wake early to tackle a flora walk with a guide, and then set off to see where Ben and his chefs 'shop'. He will introduce you to his pigs and chickens and walk you around his vegetable garden (not Babylonstoren, he laughingly claims), and tell you about the local suppliers they support - for quail, charcuterie, cheese and butter.

Grootbos is gorgeous gourmet dining. Guests return for horse riding, whale watching and for more of this happy, humble gentleman's fabulous food.

INGREDIENTS

Shiitake carpaccio
150g fresh shiitake

Shiitake pâté
50g onion, chopped
1 clove garlic, chopped
20ml olive oil
2 sprigs thyme
150g fresh shiitake
120ml white wine
120ml cream
100g cream cheese
salt

Pickled shiitake
120g sugar
240ml white wine vinegar
240ml water
1 bay leaf
6 peppercorns
pinch of turmeric
pinch of dried tarragon
150g fresh shiitake

Braised shiitake
20ml olive oil
100g fresh shiitake
20ml white wine vinegar

METHOD

Shiitake carpaccio
Layer the shiitake on top of each other and roll in clingwrap. Freeze the roll and, when ready to use, slice very thinly on a slicer.

Shiitake pâté
Fry the onion and garlic in the olive oil with the thyme. When the onion is nice and golden brown, add the shiitake. After frying the shiitake, add the wine and cook until reduced. Now add the cream and cream cheese, and cook until the cream cheese is totally melted. Transfer to a blender and blitz to a smooth consistency. Season to taste and transfer to a piping bag.

Pickled shiitake
Place all the ingredients except the shiitake in a saucepan and bring to a simmer, then add the shiitake and simmer for another two minutes. Transfer the mix to a sterilised jar.

Braised shiitake
Place oil and shiitake in a very hot frying pan. Slightly brown the shiitake, then deglaze the pan with the vinegar. Remove from heat and keep for when plating.
Serves about 10

"Take one ingredient and pull it apart – see how much you can do with it."
CHEF BEN CONRADIE

Plate of shiitake

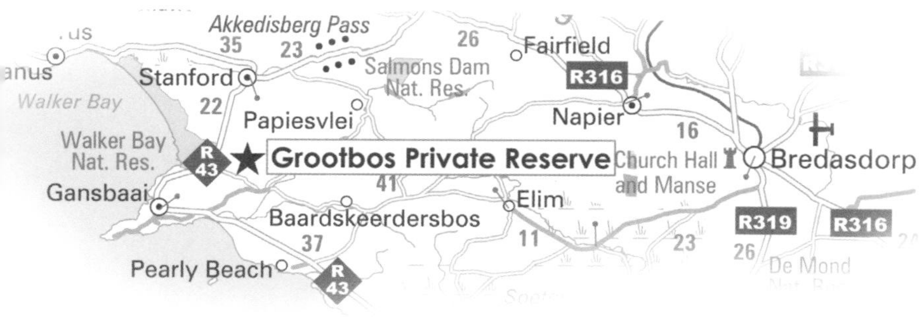

Hartford House

a magical meander into food of the future

"While there is immense attention to detail with a sense of sophistication and colonial charm, there is nothing stiff and starchy about Hartford House."

Hlatikulu Road,
Mooi River, 3300
+27 33 263 2713
www.hartford.co.za/restaurant
GPS: S29°13'15.45"
E29°56'12.65"

Take a two-hour drive from Durban or meander slowly through the KwaZulu-Natal Midlands to book into Hartford House and tick off something special on your bucket list. Unwind, relax and relish the relaxed grandeur of years gone by. Where better than in a lake suite with a private pool, at one with nature? Having pre-dinner drinks on the patio after wandering around the gorgeous gardens (where antelope insist on chewing the roses), you are likely to engage in lively conversation with international visitors, equally impressed with all on offer. Staff show genuine warmth and make everyone feel that home is where Hartford is!

All eyes have been on Chef Constantijn Hahndiek. This Capetonian had big shoes to fill, coming in hot on the heels of Jackie Cameron. He has created his own worthy footprint, studying in Devon, and working in London, Spain, France and New Zealand before heading back home.

At Hartford House bread is baked daily for each meal, from organic, stone-ground local flour, served with Mooi River butter, of course. It is this loyalty to local suppliers and their own gardens that ensures top-quality produce is the foundation of their unique daily menus. There is no room service here; just tell the obliging staff what you feel like eating, and it will appear. Personal touches are plentiful, and Tijn greets guests at their tables to unveil what they will be eating. The chicken consommé starter reflects his worth. Have his Dr Seuss green eggs and ham followed by Zulu waters hartebeest, and you will be a fan. There is a sense of fun and theatre in his presentation. While there is immense attention to detail with a sense of sophistication and colonial charm, there is nothing stiff and starchy about Hartford House.

After a sumptuous breakfast on the terrace, take a moment to meet owners Mick and Cheryl Goss, who live on the hill overlooking the stud farm, to understand their ethos. With a legacy of chefs who have all contributed to putting Hartford House firmly on the culinary map, they are there to stay. 'There is an eruption of awareness of food in South Africa,' says Tijn. Why? Because talent like this has returned home to roost.

INGREDIENTS

4 red beetroot
salt
good olive oil
2 sprigs thyme
3 tablespoons thick Greek yoghurt
juice of 1 orange
1 log chevin goat's cheese
3 tablespoons double cream
2 slices brioche
50ml red wine vinegar
20ml honey
1 sprig lavender
1 star anise
1 candy-striped pink beetroot
1 golden beetroot

METHOD

Place three of the red beetroot on a sheet of tinfoil. Sprinkle salt and olive oil over the beetroot and place the sprigs of thyme on top. Wrap up tightly so that it will steam, and place this parcel in a preheated 180°C oven for 45 minutes, until a knife pushes through the beetroot easily and it is cooked.

Peel the beetroot, quarter two of them and place the cubes on a tray, drizzling the leftover juices and oil from inside the parcel over them.

Place the remaining beetroot in a blender and blend on a high speed until smooth. Add yoghurt, season to taste and blend again, adding a little bit of fresh orange juice to liven it up.

Leave the goat's cheese at room temperature for the better part of an hour, then place it in a mixing bowl and add the cream, beating with a whisk to fluff it up until it is nice and aerated.

Juice the raw red beetroot, drizzle this over the brioche and crush up the brioche into bright purple crumbs. Season again and place in a lukewarm oven to dry out until it has a nice crumbly texture.

Place the vinegar, honey, lavender and star anise in a small saucepan on the stove, bring to a quick boil and remove.

Slice the pink beetroot thinly on a slicer and drizzle a little of the lavender dressing over the slices – but not too early or you will lose the lovely pattern.

Slice the golden beetroot thinly, squeeze a little orange juice over it and drizzle with olive oil.

PLATING

Spread some of the purée on the plate, followed by a nice roche (round) of the soft goat's cheese. Place the warm beetroot wedges alongside the goat's cheese, and stand the beetroot slices up against these. Sprinkle the beetroot crumble off to the side and then drizzle a little of the leftover lavender dressing on the plate. Garnish with beetroot leaves and any other bitter little shoots you enjoy.

Serves 4

Earth and beets

il Leone Mastrantonio

simple yet sophisticated and sincere Italian array

22 Cobern Street,
Green Point, Cape Town, 8005
+27 21 421 0071
www.mastrantonio.com/
il-leone-mastrantonio
GPS: S33°54'51.94"
E18°25'08.09"

Sited on a corner in fashionable Green Point, with a terrace that takes advantage of the Cape summer, il Leone is an elegant Italian ristorante. There is a relaxed ambience that can become noisy as the generous space is not overloaded with fabric to absorb sound. Considerate, professional service is consistent. Before you start your feast, visit the cellar to pick your bottle or take time to read through the wine list that reflects local and Italian wines.

The cold and hot starters offer plenty of options. The salad, soup, pasta, fish and chicken are all on a par, but the dishes that are on everyone's lips are the risottos, especially the seasonal porcini risotto, and the penne gamberetti (baby prawns served in olive oil with fresh tomato, cream, garlic and chilli sauce). When asked about their dish of choice, regulars reel off a list.

This classic, up-market restaurant also offers delicious desserts.

"...the dishes that are the talk of the town are the risottos..."

il Tartufo

a traditional trattoria

Hutton Court,
1 Summit Road,
Corner Jan Smuts Avenue,
Hyde Park, 2196
+27 11 788 8948
www.tartufo.co.za
GPS: S26°07'43.08"
E28°01'59.08"

If you're dreaming of an Italian gourmet experience, this is the perfect place to start your journey. This culinary gem has always served authentic regional Italian fare. Located in a small retail and office complex, il Tartufo has informal seating outside and a dark wooden, retro-style interior with red and green accent walls, and prints of Italian icons inside.

Sophia Loren would approve as serving anything less than authentic food is not acceptable to executive chef Omar Scarabello, who has worked in Michelin-starred restaurants around the world. His only concession to the South African palate is to double his pasta portions.

From a young age, Omar learned traditional Italian cooking secrets while working in his grandmother's restaurant, and still today he draws inspiration from his childhood memories. His gnocco fritto bread is freshly made, and not to be missed. Omar moved to South Africa in 2012 and has been making a name for himself for not only serving firm favourites but adding some lesser-known regional dishes to the menu. Patrons enjoy his charisma as he ventures out of the kitchen to greet diners.

The menu changes every three months but Omar uses his 'specials' blackboard to test new – and sometimes daring – dishes before adding them to the menu. His philosophy is simple: not too many elements on the plate and a maximum of six ingredients per dish.

'I bring wholesome Italian flavours to the table, with some added excitement – like the polenta gnocchi served with guinea fowl sauce. My philosophy is seasonal, fresh and good quality ingredients. I like to keep an empty freezer!'

Indochine

Pan-Asian fine dining

Delaire Graff Estate, Helshoogte Road, Stellenbosch, 7600
+27 21 885 8160
www.delaire.co.za/dining/indochine
GPS: S33°55'14.91" E18°55'08.92"

Indochine restaurant on the Delaire Graff Estate in Stellenbosch is special from start to finish. It is not just the view of the Banhoek valley and Simonsberg mountains; here all your senses will be switched on.

On arrival at the restaurant, take a moment to appreciate the swirling metallic bird sculpture above. Copper tables glint in the sun by day; by night the ambience is simply breathtaking. There is no end to the detail. It's interesting to note that chef Virgil Kahn originally wanted to be an architect before he chose food as a career. He loves the plants and gardens, and using his hands ... and he uses them well. His Asian influences were gleaned at the elbow of Quon, now head chef at Kitima, when they were working together at the Westin sushi bar. He enjoyed exposure to Japanese cuisine at Nobu, then working overseas with Thai women, learning their traditions. These he likes to marry with the history of Cape Malay cuisine through spices, and to see the flavour of the Cape shining through.

The kitchen ethos is relaxed, with the staff being very involved – all ideas are pooled and Virgil ensures that recognition is given. As a family man at home he loves comfort food. His favourite restaurants for special occasions are The Test Kitchen and Greenhouse, as he loves their refined style. This humble man is very proud of his accolades, and aims to be in the top 10 restaurants in the country ... and in the world.

You will struggle to decide what to order off Virgil's innovative menu. His cured linefish salad is delicious and unpretentious. The main course of guinea fowl and green melon is out of this world and works well with a side dish of broccoli and shiitake mushrooms. The dessert of beetroot and chocolate crumble with tonka bean ice cream, beetroot and lime doughnut is truly a treat.

The gardens at Delaire Graff form the foundation of his philosophy of farm to plate. About 95% of the salad leaves served come from the greenhouse. In spite of already using fresh and organic ingredients, future plans will see Virgil striving to be more organic. He would also like to see the restaurants at Delaire Graff collaborate more, and to serve food tapas-style. Watch this space!

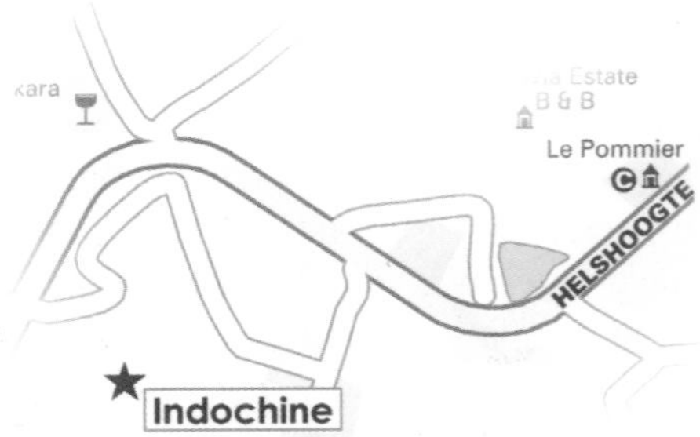

INGREDIENTS

Salad

cucumber ribbons
coconut shavings
black sesame seeds
fresh mint leaves
fresh coriander leaves
fresh basil leaves

Coconut dressing

250ml coconut milk
1 clove garlic, chopped
1 teaspoon sesame oil
fish sauce to taste
2 teaspoons palm sugar
juice of 2 limes

METHOD

First, peel the cucumber, cut it into ribbons with a peeler and set aside. Toast a handful of desiccated coconut shavings in a frying pan and set aside.

To make the dressing, mix all the dressing ingredients in a bowl and check the seasoning.

To assemble the salad, mix the cucumber ribbons, coconut shavings, black sesame seeds, mint, coriander and basil, and serve with the dressing.

"The kitchen ethos is relaxed, with the staff being very involved..."

Virgil Kahn's spring coconut salad

Jordan Restaurant

2016/2017 Gourmet Guide

a reflection of the seasons plated to perfection

Stellenbosch Kloof Road,
Stellenbosch, 7600
+27 21 881 3441
www.jordanwines.com/dine-with-us/jordan-restaurant
GPS: S33°56'35.64"
E18°44'41.87"

Jordan Wine Estate in Stellenbosch makes the most of its idyllic position. With one look at the setting on the lake when on the approach road, you can feel the layers of stress ebb away. The terrace overlooks the lake and vineyards, and inside the look is modern, cool and uncluttered. There is also the tasting room, where you can sip superlative Jordan wines, and The Bakery, which, with its relaxed ambience and lively touches of red, allows guests to eat light meals alfresco on the deck. Recently added luxury suites have increased the options and made this an ideal gourmet getaway.

'I get inspiration from the people I work with, who are full of ideas, and from the produce. There is new produce in our kitchen daily, and there is new produce constantly available. I love everything that is fresh and in season. Sustainability is everything. In South Africa we experience the necessity to have sustainable practices. It is very important, where possible, to use ingredients that are farmed and fished in a sustainable manner.'

At George Jardine's restaurant nothing changes other than the ingredients, which are simply combined and beautifully plated. The standards and service remain supreme and guests return for his delicious food. That is how he wants it to be described: 'Rather than labelling my restaurant as a particular style, I just want people to say that the food is delicious!'

George enjoys entertaining in his home and being entertained in friends' homes, dining out at Chefs Warehouse & Canteen and Burrata in Cape Town, and at Overture in Stellenbosch. His recently opened restaurant, Jardine's, in Stellenbosch, is hot news.

INGREDIENTS

Soufflé base

6 egg yolks
50g castor sugar
20g cake flour
250ml milk
5ml honey
2g poppy seeds

Soufflé

50g soufflé base
10g soft butter
20g brown sugar
100g egg whites
30g sugar

METHOD

Soufflé base

In a large bowl, combine the egg yolks, castor sugar and flour. Bring the milk to the boil. Pour it over the egg mixture, whisking to combine quickly. Return the mixture to the saucepan and cook over a low heat until it thickens to a paste. Stir continuously. Do not let this mixture boil, but make sure the flour is cooked out for at least five minutes. Once it has thickened, remove from the heat, mix in the honey and poppy seeds, and chill as quickly as possible.

Soufflé

Preheat the oven to 180°C. Brush two 13cm ramekins or moulds evenly with the soft butter. Place in the fridge to set slightly, then brush again with butter. Coat the buttered moulds with the brown sugar, making sure there are no gaps. In a large bowl, whisk the egg whites with the sugar until semi-stiff peaks have formed. Fold the egg whites into the base mixture, making sure they are well incorporated, but do not overmix. Pour the mixture into the two moulds. Scrape off the top with a palette knife to make it even, and clean any excess mix off the moulds. Place the soufflés in the oven and bake for 10 minutes. Serve them immediately.

Honey and poppy seed soufflé

"I love everything that is fresh and in season."

Chef George Jardine

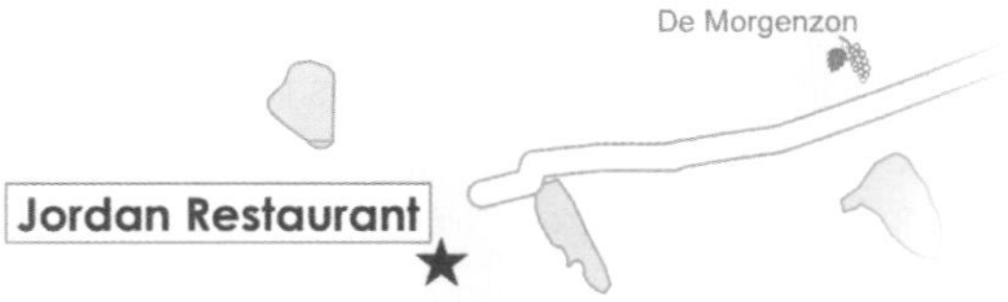

The Kitchen and The Dining Room

food with soul

111 Sir Lowry Road,
Woodstock, Cape Town, 7925
+27 21 462 2201
www.lovethekitchen.co.za
GPS: S33°55'39.03"
E18°26'17.34"

Karen Dudley built up a loyal and devoted following with her eat-on-the-go, filled-with-love eatery, The Kitchen, on Sir Lowry Road in Woodstock. She deservedly found fame when Michelle Obama visited. Her fans were then allowed to fall in love again, with more time, seats and opening hours to savour her vibey, soulful food. The restaurant next door but one is aptly called The Dining Room. Here the decor is similar but simpler, with fewer of Granny's knick-knacks taking up space on the backdrop of charcoal walls, but nostalgia is still evident. Clever, cost-effective tables are upcycled from parquet flooring. The ambience is slightly more subdued and sedate, but the noise levels rise many decibels when the restaurant is full, as it is here that people come to congregate and have a good time over delicious food.

Small, intimate tables with effervescent service and punchy flavour combinations make this a must-try, in spite of the area being quiet in the evenings. The daily menu is unceremoniously inscribed on a roll of brown paper. There is a solo dish of the day, plus a vegetarian option. It could feature a memorable seared salmon with a Tokyo wasabi dressing, black rice, beetroot with caraway, rocket and broccoli if you are lucky. Try their home-made cordial and choice of two desserts or cakes. Open for a three-course dinner on Tuesdays and Thursdays, for which there is a list of faithful followers who book regularly. Other nights it is booked for private parties. If you love what is on offer at either The Kitchen or The Dining Room, you will love both of Karen's recipe books – *The Kitchen*, and *Another Week in the Kitchen*. Hopefully she is penning The Dining Room recipes too.

The Kitchen at Maison

from the land to grand, yet always relaxed

Maison Estate, R45,
Franschhoek, 7690
+27 21 876 2116
www.maisonestate.co.za/
the-kitchen-restaurant
GPS: S33°53'10.24"
E19°04'38.45"

From the moment the fascinating origami-style light fittings in animal shapes beckon in the breeze to the chickens coming to cluck around your feet, you will feel at home. Chris Weylandt's home in Franschhoek has a restaurant that showcases his style and the talents of chef Arno Janse van Rensburg. You can sit outside on the patio and savour the vineyard views, or do a little window shopping on the quiet. Naturally, the furniture and tableware are simple and stylish.

Arno Janse van Rensburg started here when the restaurant opened in 2011, as did most of the team. They source 95% of their produce locally, like asparagus from the farm down the road. Arno gets his inspiration from nature and the surroundings, where he finds it easy to be creative.

The influences of his childhood and family are given good mileage on his menu. During his growing-up years they would fish, hunt, dive and pursue other outdoor activities, so it's no surprise to see that he makes his own sausage, loves charcuterie and likes cooking seafood. As the seasons change, so does his menu. A mid-year break in 2015 gave him the chance to work in Denmark, where he loved their wholesome approach to food and the fact that they often only present three or four ingredients on a plate.

Try the octopus and white anchovy with black garlic aioli, caper spice and apple, or the tempura crayfish tail with a Huguenot custard and tomato tartar to start. Take a gap before salivating on the suckling pig and rabbit for mains. If in season, treat yourself to the spectacular pea and chocolate mousse dessert. When peas are growing prolifically, Arno challenges the palate of the average diner with this dessert. The sweetness comes from the peas, a little bit of basil gel in between the two layers gives it definition, and then the chocolate component balances the two. Words cannot do it justice!

Ask him about his top-of-mind restaurants and he will tell you Maria's in the Gardens and Palma in Bree Street. However, here is another young chef who prefers to cook and eat at his Cape Town home, preferably at the braai.

Octopus with Sriracha, Brussels sprouts, mullet, aioli, lemon and basil

INGREDIENTS

Mullet

150g mullet/mackerel
1 cup salt
1 cup vinegar
1/4 cup sugar
4 tablespoons canola oil
80g aioli

Sriracha

800g jalapeño, chopped
190g garlic, chopped
110g ginger, chopped
600ml apple cider vinegar
100g molasses
140g honey
80g salt
1g Xanten gum
1/3 cup oil

Octopus

1 onion, chopped
1 head garlic, chopped
fresh ginger, same size as garlic head, chopped
1 chilli, chopped
2 bay leaves
10 white peppercorns
10 sprigs thyme
1kg octopus
300g Brussels sprouts
20g Sriracha emulsion
fresh lemon juice
25 basil leaves

METHOD

Mullet

Clean the mullet, debone, cover in salt and set aside for two months. After two months in salt, place in the vinegar and sugar and leave for three months. After three months in vinegar, vac seal it in the oil for three months before use. When ready to use, the mullet is skinned and chopped and mixed with aioli.

Sriracha

Blend the Sriracha ingredients and ferment for four weeks. When fermented, cook up and use.

Octopus

Place the onion, garlic, ginger, chilli, bay leaves, white peppercorns and thyme in a saucepan on high heat. Wash the octopus and suckers well, letting it drip dry in a steaming tray. Place the octopus, large side first, into the saucepan and cover immediately. Turn the heat down to a low flame and cook for about 40 minutes until almost soft. Let it steam inside the saucepan off the heat until tender.

Quickly sauté the Brussels sprouts in a little oil in a very hot pan until bright green, about one minute. Add the octopus to the pan and let it sit for two minutes. Serve the octopus and Brussels sprouts with Sriracha, mullet and aioli, and finish the plate with a squeeze of fresh lemon. Garnish with basil leaves.
Serves 6

Kitima Restaurant

the infusion of traditional Thai with all of Asia

140 Main Road,
Hout Bay,
Cape Town, 7806
+27 21 790 8004
www.kitima.co.za
GPS: S34°01'56.22"
E18°21'23.54"

Set on the main road of the sleepy seaside village of Hout Bay, Kitima has turned the tables on the ghost reputed to reside in the historic Kronendal homestead. In the 1800s the owner's daughter, Elsa Cloete, was forbidden to marry her soldier lover, and died of a broken heart. A table is laid each night for them. She, like the local residents of the self-proclaimed Republic of Hout Bay, are happy that locals and visitors alike make the trek to experience the finest Thai/Asian cuisine that the Cape has on offer.

Declared a national monument in 1961, this Cape Dutch house has been transformed with glamorous and opulent Thai decor. The red walls and gilt of the Raya Lounge and bar area form a dramatic backdrop for those wanting just the cocktail and canapé menus. When ready to experience the vision of proprietor Kitima Sukonpongpao and the talent of chef Kuan Lai and his team, move into the up-market and elegant dining rooms for the à la carte and set menus. The main focus is on Royal Thai cuisine, which, like the gracious building, can be traced back to the 17th century.

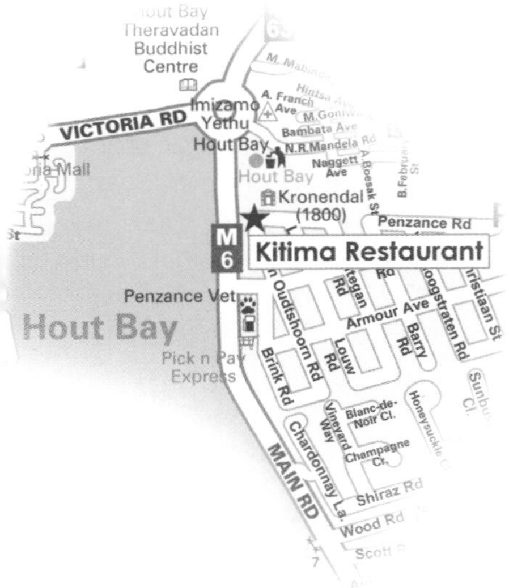

'My inspiration and passion come from various times within my life but, as of late, the drive that Kitima has keeps me pushing harder and harder every day to deliver the best Thai/Asian food that Africa has seen. I favour all the aromatic spices from my country. I truly am grateful for the abundance of herbs and spices I grew up with. I strongly believe in seasonality and sustainability. We have our own compost machine – this caters for the several herb gardens we have on and off the premises. A large portion of my day is spent cultivating a variety of herbs needed for our cooking. Kitima's personal residence has several ducks and chickens where we collect their eggs, fresh for service. Where I can, I look to minimise wastage and look towards a more sustainable business,' says Kuan Lai.

Kitima has a winter menu, a summer menu, a set menu that changes quarterly, and a popular Sunday buffet. Kuan likes to cook at home for a special occasion. 'I love to feed people and watch their reactions as they take their first bite. Casually, I just enjoy street food – the atmosphere, sounds and aromas where you can meander through the stalls, sampling all that is on offer.'

There is a lot on offer at Kitima, not just Thai – from Indian curries to Indonesian fare, from sushi to dim sum. All yum sum. If overwhelmed by choice, make a date with one of the lauded Asian duck dishes.

INGREDIENTS

Orange saffron glaze

500ml orange juice (pure fruit juices blend)
500ml freshly squeezed orange juice
50g lemon juice
100g sugar
0.001g saffron thread (Spanish)
5g star anise
5g stick cinnamon
3g bay leaves
10ml Cointreau
50g butter

Roast duck

120g soy bean paste
30g garlic
50g ginger
5g bay leaves
30g sugar
60g salt
10g five spice powder
2.5kg whole free-range duck
1 bamboo skewer
50g maltose sugar
1 litre water
200ml red vinegar

Confit duck leg

4 duck legs
10g five spice powder
60g salt
300g free-range duck fat
15g star anise
50g garlic
50g ginger
5g black peppercorns
30g spring onion

METHOD

Orange saffron glaze

Combine orange juice, lemon juice and sugar, and bring to the boil. Add spices, simmer for 30 minutes to reduce and form a glaze, then add bay leaves and Cointreau. Add a knob of butter for a glossy finish.

Roast duck

Combine the dry marinade ingredients (soy bean paste, garlic, ginger, bay leaves, sugar, salt and five spice powder) in a small bowl and thoroughly rub inside the duck cavity. Close belly opening with the bamboo skewer.

Combine the coating syrup ingredients (maltose sugar, water and vinegar) in a large saucepan or wok and bring to the boil. Coat the entire duck with the syrup, then drain and pat dry. Hang the duck by a string in a cool place until the skin is taut and dry – four hours to overnight.

Preheat the oven to 200°C. Place duck, breast side up, on a rack in a tinfoil-lined roasting pan. Roast for 30 minutes on each side. Turn duck breast side up again and roast for a further 10 minutes. Remove duck from oven and let it stand for 10 minutes before serving.

Confit duck leg

Place the duck legs in a roasting tray and sprinkle with the five spice powder and salt. Cover the tray with clingwrap and chill in the fridge overnight. Preheat the oven to 200°C. Heat a heavy-based frying pan over a low to medium heat, place the duck legs in the pan and cover them completely in the free-range duck fat. Add the star anise, garlic, ginger, peppercorns and spring onion. Cook in the oven for two hours.

Heat a little duck fat in a frying pan over a high heat. Add the cooked duck legs, skin side down, and fry for two to three minutes, or until the skin is crispy.

'I love to feed people and watch their reactions as they take their first bite.

Chef Kuan Lai

Kloof Street House

enigmatic and alluring

30 Kloof Street, Gardens,
Cape Town, 8001
+27 21 423 4413
www.kloofstreethouse.co.za
GPS: S33°55'41.84"
E18°24'44.12"

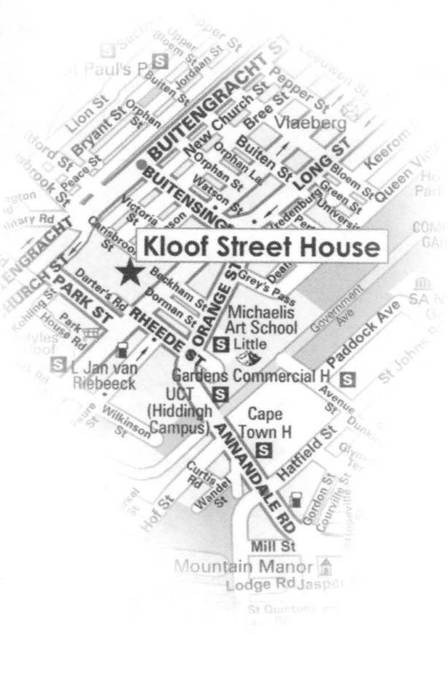

So the name is a giveaway. This character Victorian house sits in the burgeoning gastronomy mile of Kloof Street at the foot of Table Mountain in Cape Town.

Start your romantic tryst with one of their celebrated cocktails in the garden, camouflaged by trees twinkling with fairy lights. Move inside into one of the alluring individual rooms – take a seat in the dining room or library lounge, all opulently decorated, or stay outside if the weather allows and enjoy the fairytale feeling.

The à la carte menu is comprehensive. For starters, try the pan-fried baby Patagonian calamari with aioli and harissa, or the oysters. Their salads are sublime – choose from caprese or the hero ingredients of aubergine or halloumi. For mains, most carnivore appetites will be met with their Moroccan spiced lamb rump, the osso bucco or the ostrich fillet. The baked lentil and artichoke loaf is perfect as a vegetarian option. Three desserts are on offer, or take the medley of desserts, which feeds four. Service is as effervescent as the setting, and a great addition to the menu on a Sunday is jazz.

Kurland

home from home

Kurland Hotel, The Crags,
N2, Plettenberg Bay, 6602
+27 44 534 8082
www.kurland.co.za/dining
GPS: S33°56'27.46"
E23°29'11.13"

One can be forgiven for thinking that Kurland in Plettenberg Bay is all about equestrian pleasures, but only if you have not experienced it. Kurland is a home from home with a feeling of authentic luxury. Family-owned and run, the staff are willing and warm and their generous yet unhurried hospitality creates a sense of being part of the family. In winter the gracious homestead is warmed by crackling fires, where guests congregate for convivial conversation; in summer they linger on the patio over elegant breakfasts, high tea or G&T, with views of the horses, award-winning roses and greenery. While the atmosphere is one of complete relaxation, there is subtle sophistication that reminds you that you are in a five-star establishment.

All 12 suites are spacious and tastefully decorated with attention to detail and fabulous views. If exclusivity is desired, the Kurland Villa is an option; set next to the polo estate, this magnificent retreat accommodates up to 16 people. You may work off the exceptional cuisine with mountain- or quad biking, horse riding or tennis.

Leon Coetzee, executive chef, started their 'come into my kitchen' philosophy. The kitchen is enjoyed by families, and children are invited in to learn how to make cupcakes and sweet treats, but only after getting to grips with Leon's pride and joy – his herb garden. He started it upon arrival at Kurland five years ago, and his Gourmet Garden menu bears testament to the fruits of his labour. Lunches and dinners see small, select and seasonal menus that pay homage not only to the herb garden, but also to the best of organic suppliers in the area. His warm artichoke salad with confit tomato, feta and honey mustard dressing is a winner, and his grilled aubergine with wild mushroom ragout, rocket and Parmesan salad with an aged balsamic reduction is a highlight on the ever-changing seasonal menu. Local wines are personally recommended with meals, rather than having a lengthy wine list from which to choose.

'The nature and quality of life keeps people here in Plett. As a chef I am humble – no chef is bigger than the game. I love changing the menu daily to suit the preferences of guests, which keeps it creative and personal, and I also love interacting with guests.'

"As a chef I am humble – no chef is bigger than the game."

Chef Leon Coetzee

INGREDIENTS

Ravioli dough

500g cake flour
pinch of salt
6 whole eggs
4 egg yolks
2 tablespoons water
2 tablespoons olive oil

Ravioli filling

300g freshwater prawns
300g fresh Norwegian salmon
3 spring onions, chopped
salt and pepper
1 clove garlic, chopped

Oriental vegetables

2 carrots
1 baby marrow
½ red pepper
½ yellow pepper
1 red onion
80g red cabbage, sliced

Vermouth velouté

7 shallots, diced
600ml vermouth (extra dry)
1 litre fish stock
1 litre fresh cream
30g unsalted butter
40g flour

METHOD

Ravioli dough

Combine the flour and salt in the food processor and mix well. While the food processor is running, add the eggs, egg yolks, water and oil and process until all is combined like a dough. Knead well, wrap in clingwrap and put in the fridge for 15 minutes.

Ravioli filling

Combine all the ingredients in a blender but do not blend until smooth – maintain its chunky textures. Once your dough is ready, slide through a pasta machine on levels one through to seven. Place the pasta sheets on a surface covered in flour. Use a 10cm ring cutter to cut out the shapes. Roll a tablespoon of the filling mixture into a small ball. Place that in the centre of the pasta ring, dip your fingertips in water and wet the edge of the pasta ring. Place the other pasta ring on top and seal each 'parcel'. Continue until the filling is finished. Place the raviolis on a floured tray and refrigerate for 15 minutes.

Prepare a pot of boiling water on the stove with two tablespoons of oil. Place the raviolis in the water and cook until tender (around seven minutes).

Oriental vegetables

Using a mandoline, slice the carrots and baby marrow thinly, about half a centimetre thick, and then put all the vegetables together and slice them in a julienne style. Fry in a wok or pan until al dente.

Vermouth velouté

Mix the shallots and vermouth together in a copper-bottomed pan. Reduce the vermouth to a jam. Add the fish stock and reduce by half. Add the cream and bring to the boil, then turn down to a simmer. Mix the butter and flour to form a roux. Slowly add this to the simmering sauce and cook to a consistent texture. Strain and cool. Serve warm. Do not boil again as it will split. For a variation, try using Chablis (sweet wine) instead of the vermouth.

Ravioli of salmon and freshwater prawns, oriental vegetables and a Vermouth velouté

La Boheme Wine Bar & Bistro

grab a front-row seat for generous food, good times, great value

341 Main Road,
Sea Point, Cape Town, 8005
+27 21 434 8797
www.labohemebistro.co.za
GPS: S33°54'50.95"
E18°23'29.13"

Sitting plum on the pavement on the bustling Sea Point strip is La Boheme, where patrons enjoy casual, comforting bistro fare – inside or alfresco – in this vibey Atlantic seaside suburb.

Painas Muzika's home is in Zimbabwe, where he trained as a chef before working at Simon's at Groot Constantia. He cooks homely, honest food from the heart, and favours the process of braising and slow cooking. He loves working with fresh ingredients and his favourite herbs are oregano and rosemary. His signature dish, the balsamic beef fillet with mushroom risotto and mushroom sauce, keeps regulars coming back for more. The menu follows the seasons but rings the changes weekly, and he supports local suppliers, always aiming for consistency of standards. Other favourites that seem to have found a permanent place on the portable blackboard menu are the carpaccio and paella, paying homage to the co-owner Anna Rascola's Spanish mother, who made her memorable paella for her birthday, so she decided to use the authentic family recipe and wonderful influences of her homeland in the dishes at La Boheme.

The other owner, Faisal Khakoo, is from Tanzania. You will find one of them on the floor, ensuring that patrons are well cared for, the other at their recently opened Bouchon in the Durant Cellar off Heritage Square, where international and local wines are served by the glass. Every week they open a special bottle so that guests can relish a discovery of wine. The only wine bar of its kind in Sea Point, La Boheme's wine list is extensive and reasonably priced, with more than 60 wines available by the glass.

Painas believes that a chef should constantly research and always strive to offer good value. 'Play with a combination of flavours and then come up with your own brand.' La Mouette is his favourite fine dining restaurant, and for a casual meal, Black Sheep.

Sister restaurant La Bruixa (meaning 'witch'!) is where you will get great espressos and tapas. Engruna, next door, also their baby, means 'crumbs' in Spanish. Here they serve gourmet pizzas and burgers, craft beers, wine and milkshakes. La Boheme means 'the carefree life'.

INGREDIENTS

Mushroom risotto

cooking oil
1 small onion, finely chopped
2 sticks celery, trimmed and finely chopped
500g risotto rice
$^2/_3$ cup white wine
1kg brown mushrooms
6 $^1/_3$ cups beef stock
a few sprigs of fresh chervil, tarragon or parsley leaves, picked and chopped
2 tablespoons butter
2 handfuls freshly grated Parmesan cheese
juice of 1 lemon

Mushroom sauce

$^1/_2$ onion
pinch of crushed fresh garlic
250g mushrooms
cooking oil
750ml cream
250ml beef stock
10ml soy sauce
1 lemon
salt and pepper

Balsamic beef fillet

2 x 100g medallions beef fillet per person
dash of maple syrup
dash of red wine
dash of balsamic vinegar

Balsamic beef fillet with mushroom risotto and mushroom sauce

METHOD

Mushroom risotto

In a large saucepan, heat the cooking oil and add the onion and celery. Slowly fry without colouring for at least 10 minutes. Turn the heat down, add the rice, and give it a stir with a wooden spoon (it is essential to use a wooden spoon when stirring risotto). Stir in the white wine and keep stirring until the liquid has cooked into the rice. Add the mushrooms and stock. Turn the heat down to a simmer, stirring and massaging the starch out of the rice. For al dente risotto, cook for 12–15 minutes, or for cooked through risotto about 20 minutes. Add the herbs. Remove the risotto from the heat and check the seasoning. Stir in the butter and the Parmesan cheese. Squeeze lemon juice over and serve.

Mushroom sauce

Sauté the onion, garlic, and mushrooms in a little oil. Add half of the cream and all the stock, and reduce by half. Add the rest of the cream and reduce until nappe (the consistency to coat a wooden spoon). Add soy sauce, and a squeeze of lemon juice. Season to taste.

Balsamic beef fillet

Seal the fillet in the pan for two minutes and then add remaining ingredients. Cook to your preference.
Serves 4–6

La Colombe

French with Asian touches of playfulness – food to remember for years to come

"The setting is uncontrived, almost devoid of decor. Here it is all about the food."

Silvermist Wine Estate,
Constantia Main Road,
Constantia, Cape Town, 7806
+27 21 795 0125
www.lacolombe.co.za
GPS: S 34°00'43.47"
E18°24'08.78"

La Colombe's natural new home in the Silvermist Organic Wine Estate in Constantia equates to executive chef Scot Kirton's culinary talent and the high level of service. The setting is uncontrived, almost devoid of decor. Here it is all about the food.

You may start your adventure with a sealed tin, which you open to discover a beautifully plated tuna tataki inside. Or a sphere that is served on a bed of pebbles that explodes when you bite into it. There is always an element of surprise and an inkling of Scot's personality peeking through.

'Inspirations come from many sources; many dishes are inspired by the change of seasons. Different crockery also inspires new dishes; I am currently working on a sea urchin dish inspired by a porcelain sea urchin shell I found in Simon's Town. I enjoy Asian ingredients as they add intense flavour to dishes. Currently my favourite dish is the Asian-style scallops and pork belly with corn, kimchi, aubergine, lemongrass and ginger. The fattiness in the pork cuts through the subtle scallops perfectly. All our food is seasonal, and this inspires most menu changes. We are also very aware of sustainability and do our part in serving sustainable fish, etc. We try to change at least one dish every two weeks. It often takes 10 to 15 attempts on a dish before we get it right.'

If the scallops and pork are not on the menu, celebrate gastronomy with the Alaskan snow crab with yellowtail ceviche, or finish your feast with the dessert of raspberry and chocolate stracciatella ... or the rose and coconut panna cotta with cashew, lime and orange blossom. There is a gourmand menu paired with fine and rare wines, or the classic and vegetarian menus to choose from, for lunch and dinner.

Globally recognised Kirton trained at Haute Cabrière in Franschhoek and at Gordon Ramsay's Savoy Grill in London. He returned to South Africa to cook under mentor Luke Dale-Roberts at La Colombe, and then beside him, which he claims shaped his culinary expertise and personal style. No surprise that he is now mentoring and shaping his own team of professionals. Also no surprise that Scot favours the Greenhouse or The Test Kitchen for a special occasion, The Pot Luck Club or Chefs Warehouse & Canteen for a more casual meal.

INGREDIENTS

Quail breast
2g salt
20g butter
1 clove garlic, crushed
2 sprigs thyme
1 quail (legs removed)

Confit quail leg
2g salt
sprig thyme
2 quail legs
300ml oil

Foie gras
30g A-grade deveined foie gras, scored

Caramelised brioche
300g honey
300g water
1 vanilla pod
300g brioche, torn into chunks

Almond purée
300g roasted almonds
600g milk
30g honey
salt to taste

Candied almonds
50g whole almonds, roasted
30g sugar
2g salt
100ml Amaretto

Rum-braised pineapple
750ml dark rum
100g dark sugar
600g orange juice
1 star anise
1 stick cinnamon
zest of 1 lemon
1 vanilla pod
3 pineapples, peeled

Pineapple purée
1 braised pineapple
50ml thyme balsamic

Buchu jus
100ml ruby port
200ml demi-glace
1g dried buchu leaves
knob of butter

METHOD

Quail breast
Mix the salt with the butter, garlic and thyme and stuff into the quail cavity. Vac pack on full and sous-vide at 55°C for 15 minutes before sealing in hot oil.

Confit quail leg
Rub salt and thyme on the quail legs and confit at 70°C for two hours.

Foie gras
Season the foie gras well and fry on high heat until core temperature of 55°C is reached.

Caramelised brioche
Mix honey, water and vanilla together. Briefly dip the brioche chunks into the syrup and spread out on a baking tray. Bake for six minutes at 180°C. Turn and bake again until caramelised and golden.

Almond purée
Roast the nuts and boil the milk. Place both in a blender while very hot and blend until smooth. Season with honey and salt to taste.

Candied almonds
Toss the almonds in the sugar, salt and amaretto mix, spread out on a baking tray and roast for eight minutes at 180°C.

Rum-braised pineapple
Boil all the ingredients, except pineapples, together. Add the pineapples and cover in a cartouche. Braise at 160°C for half an hour or until tender. Allow to cool, brunoise the pineapple and reserve in a little of the liquid.

Pineapple purée
Heat a pan until hot, roughly chop the pineapple (retain some of the pineapple for garnish) and fry until dry. Deglaze with thyme balsamic and cook out. Blend until smooth.

Buchu jus

Reduce the port to a glaze. Add the demi-glace and reduce to sauce consistency. Sprinkle in the buchu and steep for 10 minutes. Strain and mount with a knob of butter to finish.

PLATING

Arrange all ingredients on the plate in your own creative way, adding the foie gras and buchu jus last.

Quail with foie gras, almond, pineapple and buchu

La Cucina di Ciro

celebrate the art of fine dining and la dolce vita

43 7th Avenue,
Parktown North, 2193
+27 11 442 5187
www.lacucinadiciro.co.za
GPS: S26°08'40.93"
E28°01'47.68"

Ciro's may be famous for fresh pasta, but there are many other reasons, like sterling service, to put La Cucina di Ciro on your speed dial. Inspired by Italy, this gem in Parktown North has been drawing regulars for many years. You may witness a group of businessmen sealing a few deals, friends celebrating a birthday, or regulars coming back for the warm welcome and guarantee of the best that Italy can offer. By night it turns into a romantic rendezvous enhanced by the low lights and the spell of background jazz. Monogrammed white linen napkins illustrate standards and attention to detail.

Chef patron Ciro Molinaro, who has been cooking for more than 30 years, believes in using what nature offers, and while organic food is more expensive, he believes one should eat less, better, and waste less too. Here they work with what is available and in season, changing the small menu monthly, except for their legendary duck, which by demand remains a feature. Self-motivated Ciro enjoys cooking and people, and laughingly calls himself a food psychologist. 'You have to understand people. Everyone is a food critic and many people have food intolerances, so you have to be flexible.' He knows and encourages the ethos of coming together to enjoy food and people around a table. His well-picked yet small wine list shows his ethos of good entertaining.

If you don't like helping yourself, one of the attentive staff will make a selection of the antipasto buffet for primi. Follow that with in-house-made pasta like the fettucine tossed with fresh tomato concasse, mint and olive oil topped with crumbed spicy prawns. For secondi, try the catch of the day (seafood is a speciality) and don't leave without enjoying dolce as all desserts are delectable.

If you are looking for a vegetarian experience, then pop into The Pudding Shop next door, run by Ciro's wife - open for breakfast and lunch and favoured by vegetarians.

La Mouette Restaurant

modern French cuisine with strong South African influences

78 Regent Road, Sea Point,
Cape Town, 8005
+27 21 433 0856
www.lamouette-restaurant.co.za
GPS: S33°55'16.66"
E18°22'57.44"

At the one end of Sea Point's Main Road there is a Tudor-style house that is the perfect stage for classically trained English chef Henry Vigar to strut his stuff. For cocktails to craft beers, romantic trysts to large groups, guests gather in summer in the courtyard at the fountain or in winter take refuge at the fireplace inside, to experience the à la carte or tasting menu.

There is a hint of the Mediterranean in the menu, and Henry's signature dish is the charred sole with charcoal mayonnaise. Henry is married to a South African, and local influence is reflected in the produce and seasonality. He loves experimenting with new techniques and is forever exploring the wonders of local and small suppliers. His menus change regularly, about every six weeks, based on the changing of the seasons and the produce each season brings.

'Growing up in England, and spending a lot of time in my youth in Europe for holidays, has taught me the importance of respect for seasonal produce. I try to mirror that in my seasonally inspired menus. My inspiration comes from a number of things, which include my past travelling experiences, seasonality, reading cookery books, as well as nature.' Vigar enjoys culinary travel to get inspired and to see what is happening, especially in London and European cities, where he also buys books that inspire him.

"My inspiration comes from a number of things, which include my past travelling experiences, seasonality, reading cookery books, as well as nature."

CHEF HENRY VIGAR

His favourite staple ingredients are onions and tomatoes, the base of almost everything he likes to cook. Proteins he favours are fish and duck, and all sorts of local cheese. 'We have some magnificent cheese currently being produced in the Cape. I always aim to reflect sustainability in an alliance with my seasonal inspiration; for example, every year the countdown until tuna season is on and my supplier brings me the most amazing fresh tuna, only available in summer – you will never see tuna on my menu in winter. Sustainability is key, as well as supporting local, ethical farmers, fishermen and growers along the way.'

Charred East Coast sole

Vigar's dish to eat in his down time is a thin-crust wood-oven pizza, preferably at Massimo's in Hout Bay. For a special occasion it has to be The Test Kitchen. 'We always have a booking there waiting, even if it is six months away; it is always not only inspirational but so worth the wait.'

Waiting is one thing you are unlikely to do at La Mouette (meaning 'seagull' in French), as the service there matches the fine food.

INGREDIENTS

Charcoal oil
90g charcoal
500g pomace oil

Charcoal mayonnaise
4 egg yolks
1/2 teaspoon squid ink
2 teaspoons white balsamic vinegar
300g charcoal oil
warm water as required
pinch of salt
juice of 1/2 lemon

Umami vinaigrette
200ml ponzu
20g kombu
4 sheets nori
100ml water
50g sugar
150ml sunflower oil
10g bonito flakes
1 teaspoon cornflour

Parsnip purée
1kg parsnips, peeled and diced
1 onion, sliced
100g butter
200ml cream
200ml vegetable stock

Parsnip crisps
2 parsnips
oil for frying

Roasted parsnips
4 parsnips
salt and pepper to taste
a little olive oil

Onion ash
1 onion, finely sliced

Sole
2 fillets sole per person
salt to taste

METHOD

Charcoal oil
Barbecue the charcoal until it is white and very hot. Place the charcoal into the oil and infuse for 24 hours. Pass through muslin.

Charcoal mayonnaise
Whisk together the egg yolks, squid ink and vinegar. Slowly add the charcoal oil and continue whisking until it becomes emulsified and thick. If it's too thick, add a little bit of warm water. Season with the salt and lemon juice.

Umami vinaigrette
Combine all ingredients and heat up to 80°C. Remove from the heat and leave to infuse for an hour, then strain and thicken with a teaspoon of cornflour.

Parsnip purée
Sweat down the parnips and onion in butter for about 10 minutes. Add the cream and vegetable stock, cover with a lid and simmer for about half an hour till the parsnips are soft, checking every so often that they are not burning. Place in the blender and blend till smooth; it may require a light vegetable stock to help the blending.

Parsnip crisps
Peel parsnips and thinly slice on a mandoline. Fry at 120°C until golden.

Roasted parsnips
Peel parsnips, cut out centre root, then cut into wedges. Bring a pot of salted water to the boil, add the parsnips, cook until tender, then drain (make sure they are completely dry). Place in a baking tray in preheated oven (180°C) with salt, pepper and a bit of olive oil and roast for 15–20 minutes until they are light and crispy.

Onion ash
Place onion on a baking sheet and roast at 180°C until it is completely blackened. Place in the blender and grind until becomes a powder.

Sole
Season the sole with salt and some of the umami vinaigrette. Place under the griller and grill for two to four minutes until the fish feels cooked.

PLATING

Place the parsnip purée in the middle of the plate. Add a few dots of the charcoal mayonnaise, followed by the fish. Finish with roasted parsnips, parsnip crisps, onion ash and the umami vinaigrette.

Le Sel @ The Cradle

good food with a view

Quality country venues are hard to find, and the Cradle is a reliable option with celebrated chef Coco Reinharz, born and raised in Burundi, the Congo and Belgium, at the helm. Service here is professional and dishes have gourmet flair.

Route T9, Kromdraai Road,
Cradle of Humankind
+27 11 659 1622
www.thecradle.co.za/restaurant
GPS: S25°55'24.07"
E27°51'11.73"

The setting in the Cradle of Humankind, where the first hominid was found and one of the eight World Heritage Sites in South Africa, was designed to transport one from city life (about 45 minutes from Sandton) to the bush. This is also what makes it a popular wedding and conference venue.

The menu includes hearty bistro-style dishes, and the venue is popular for both brunch and lunch. His concept is seasonal and Pan-African, which, combined with his classical French training, makes for delicious flavour combinations and satisfying portions. For breakfast, don't miss the Belgian waffles with Chantilly cream and hot chocolate sauce, and the pumpkin, corn and feta fritters with bacon. Lunch starters include lovely combos such as beetroot and goat's cheese salad, ostrich carpaccio, and seafood spring rolls. Main courses embrace familiar favourites, including pasta, meat dishes and seafood – all beautifully plated. And the wine list is extensive.

'The food here is family-friendly, relaxed and unpretentious, with a focus on good quality ingredients. I try to reinvent old favourites and bring modern African flavours to the table.'

It's not fine dining at Le Sel @ The Cradle. If you wish to experience Coco's more refined food with lashings of fineness, visit his restaurant, Sel et Poivre at The Quatermain Premier Boutique Hotel, where more classical French fine dining is the order of the day, or his Le Petite Sel nearby at the Falstaff Superior Boutique Hotel.

The Leopard

food that touches your soul

63 4th Avenue, Melville,
Johannesburg, 2092
+27 11 482 9356
www.leopardfoodcompany.com
GPS: S26°10'30.52"
E28°00'20.78"

Eating at The Leopard is a casual affair. Sitting on the corner of 4th Avenue and 5th Street in buzzy Melville, at wooden tables with mismatched, yet comfy chairs, surrounded by Grandma's art, you can watch the world go by, sitting inside or on the pavement. Having originated in the swankier Parkhurst location, The Leopard has elevated this less up-market part of town. Service is lively and friendly. Well-informed, enthusiastic waiters who subscribe to the ethos of authenticity of the establishment take the time to explain the menu and mention their favourites. You may wish to start with the artichokes topped with mint, parsley, breadcrumbs, Parmesan and garlic. You may also wish to buy restaurateur and cookbook author Andrea Burgener's book *Lampedusa Pie* for this recipe alone. Or try the fennel, cucumber, mint and peanut salad with chilli dressing. The Pata plate, to be shared, provides another delicious course, and the Heversham smoky chicken is memorable. Add a glass of wine, sit back and relax.

The menu is small with interesting combinations, and seasonal with a great emphasis on sourcing and using the best ingredients. Andrea believes that you may need to pay more to get more, and the emphasis is on quality ingredients such as the Saldanha Bay mussels. No compromises here. Regular dishes stay on the menu due to popular demand, others change seasonally. Readers of Andrea's newspaper column will appreciate the opportunity to connect with her, and to discuss the pleasures and pitfalls of turning your passion into business. Energetic Andrea claims that she is addicted to having a restaurant. The fact that they only take 'real, live telephone bookings' tells you how genuine they are at The Leopard. They are living up to lauded expectations.

Level Four

contemporary marries classic fine dining

54 on Bath,
54 Bath Avenue, Rosebank,
Johannesburg, 2196
+27 11 344 8500
www.tsogosun.com/level-four
GPS: S26°08'44.39"
E28°02'26.05"

One may remember 54 on Bath from her Grace days, a 74-roomed hotel perfectly positioned for the business or leisure traveller in the centre of Rosebank. Here understated elegance offers a welcome as you take refuge from the hustle and bustle, alongside the Rosebank Mall and near the Gautrain, Nelson Mandela Square and Wanderers Club.

You may find it hard to tear yourself away from the Veuve Clicquot Champagne Bar, which overlooks the sunny terrace. The black-and-white decor at Level Four is contemporary and uplifting, and the white linen appropriate in this tranquil, elegant and sophisticated restaurant. The option of eating alfresco is an attractive one. Here one could cinch a great business deal, do something a little more romantic after dark or celebrate a special occasion over high tea. The menu allows for 'feed me, fill me', but concentrates on combining delicate flavours with precision and care. The wine list is extensive, as are the options by the glass.

Chef Phil de Villiers has been at Level Four since they opened. In the urban jungle he finds solace and inspiration in his rooftop garden, where he plants produce to give seasonality to his menu, which changes every six weeks. It is on the menu that he gives credit to his team – each dish on the menu has a chef's name to it as he believes good food is a team sport. It is the combination of characters and flavours that makes his food memorable. Some of these chefs have worked in Asian restaurants, so there is a discreet undertone of Asian flavours. His signature dishes are the prawns, and the braised lamb ribbetjies, an ode to his Afrikaans heritage. Their best seller is the beef fillet – no surprise, as the restaurant is a favourite of many beefy businessmen. The lobster bisque has been on the menu for more than three years to avoid a protest.

"In the urban jungle he finds solace and inspiration in his rooftop garden..."

INGREDIENTS

Calamari ceviche

8 calamari heads

Ceviche dressing

1 small red onion, grated on fine side
1 thumb-size piece of ginger, grated on fine side
2 cloves garlic, grated on fine side
1/2 teaspoon chilli flakes
1 green chilli, deseeded and finely chopped
3 tablespoons chopped fresh coriander
50ml rice vinegar
80ml mirin
300ml lime juice
50ml olive oil
25ml fish sauce

Corn salad

1 corn cob, kernels cut off the cob and blanched
1 red pepper, deseeded and brunoised
1 red onion, brunoised
10g fresh coriander, chopped

Grilled calamari

16 calamari heads, cleaned
salt to taste
1 teaspoon togarashi spice

Calamari tentacles

5 tentacles per portion
3 tablespoons seasoned flour

To finish

kimchi, chopped up and mixed with a little chopped fresh coriander
coriander shoots
nasturtiums or any edible flowers

METHOD

Calamari ceviche

Cut calamari into rings, blanch in boiling water for 30 seconds and refresh in an ice bath.

Ceviche dressing

Mix all the ingredients together. On service, mix a little of the dressing with the calamari ceviche and the corn salad and leave for five minutes to marinate.

Corn salad

Mix all the ingredients for the salad together.

Grilled calamari

Open the tubes of the calamari and score with a butter knife into diamond shapes. Blanch in boiling water for 30 seconds and refresh in an ice bath. Sprinkle with salt and a little togarashi spice.

Calamari tentacles

Coat the tentacles in flour and deep-fry in 180°C oil until crispy.

ASSEMBLY

Mix the calamari rings, the corn salad and some of the ceviche dressing and leave to marinate for five minutes. Meanwhile chargrill the calamari heads and deep fry the tentacles. Arrange on the plate and serve immediately, with kimchi, coriander shoots and nasturtium or other edible flowers.

Serves 4

Calamari variations (ceviche, grilled and fried) with corn salad and kimchi

Luce

where Italy and Japan meet and marry

The views from Hyde Park Corner are dramatic, as is the decor with lots of glass, low-hanging lighting, wooden floors and a palette of black, white and taupe colour accents. A theatrical open-plan sushi kitchen adds to the drama of the decor.

A fusion of Italian cuisine and Japanese sushi may not seem like a good marriage, but it works. Originally the hotel teamed up with the Bice international Italian franchise and Daruma, a chain started 25 years ago by Japanese chef Seishi Shibuya. A recent breaking away from Bice has meant a renaming of the restaurant. Now the restaurant can retain dishes that patrons love but the menu can expand to include some local fare. The restaurant has expanded their menu to meet the renewed demand for local beef and steaks and now showcases more meat dishes, with aged prime rib served on the bone with hand-cut chips, roasted vine tomatoes and mustard topping the charts.

Thanks to the previous Bice chefs' focus on quality ingredients, this is ingrained in the kitchen, where pasta is still home-made and everything is made from scratch. The home-made *ravioli di ricotta e spinaci al profumo di tartufo* (ricotta- and spinach-filled ravioli served in a crispy Parmesan basket with black truffles) is outstanding – not too creamy but with perfect balance of flavours. Another winner is the spaghetti alla vodka with prawns in a creamy tomato sauce.

The wine list is extensive and includes top local and Italian wines, as well as rare auction wines. Well-trained sommeliers are on hand to advise patrons on wine pairings for each course.

Southern Sun Hyde Park,
1st Road, Sandton, 2196
+27 11 341 8080
www.tsogosun.com/
luce-at-hyde-park
GPS: S26°07'28.28"
E28°01'57.68"

INGREDIENTS

170g butter
225g dark chocolate
120g white sugar
22.5g cocoa powder
8 eggs, beaten
75g cake flour

METHOD

Place the butter, chocolate, sugar and cocoa powder into a stainless steel bowl and melt over a pan of hot water (double boiler). When the chocolate mixture is well melted, stir to combine and slowly add the beaten eggs. Add sifted cake flour and stir to combine thoroughly until the mixture is smooth and velvety. It should have a dropping consistency. Grease 12 dariole moulds or ramekins with butter and dust liberally with cocoa powder. Ensure that there are no spots on the lining of the mould that have not been covered with powder, as this will result in your fondant sticking and possibly breaking. Drop enough batter into the lined moulds to fill three-quarters of the mould. This can be done beforehand and they are then baked to order, or when required, in the oven at 180°C for eight to 10 minutes. Take care not to overbake as this will fully cook the fondant, which would defeat the purpose of a hot, oozy consistency.
Serves 12

"A fusion of Italian cuisine and Japanese sushi may not seem like a good marriage, but it works."

Chocolatismo (chocolate fondant)

Magica Roma

no surprises, just magical Italian cuisine

"For Italians food is not merely about survival; it defines us, and belongs in our history and culture."

Co-owners Ezio de Biaggi and Franco Zezia

In the pedestrian suburb of Pinelands there is a small shopping centre, Central Square, that houses a big success. Ask any discerning Capetonian about their favourite go-to restaurant, and they are sure to mention Magica Roma. The decor is dated; here time has stood still. The menu is constant, other than the fresh linefish offering caught daily. Then again, who needs a menu when you can ask either of the Italian owners to suggest a meal, and you know it will be momentous? Popular for business lunches, couples and families, this Italian ristorante ticks all the boxes.

Co-owner Ezio de Biaggi explains why. 'We take inspiration from being born-and-bred Italians – our culture is naturally passionate about food and the food industry. For Italians food is not merely about survival; it defines us, and belongs in our history and culture. We harnessed our skills at catering schools in Italy and then travelled extensively, learning and working in many different countries and restaurants until we both settled in South Africa, where we hope to share our love and passion for the Mediterranean style of cooking. We work only with the freshest ingredients, from herbs to meat and fish. We prefer to rely chiefly on the quality of the ingredients rather than on elaborate preparation and presentation. Italian cuisine is characterised by its simplicity. We concentrate on mainly a Mediterranean-style cuisine with an obvious Italian influence. Since Italian cuisine varies from region to region and we both originate from different regions, we have managed to merge the different styles and recipes into our menu.'

For these Italian aficionados it is important to support local suppliers and adjust their dishes according to seasonality. They have a great respect for the environment with regard to fish and vegetables. Dishes are made to order, and modified as required, making the eating experience an individual one for each person.

Ezio and co-owner Franco Zezia both enjoy just a simple al dente pasta dish with a dash of good quality olive oil and fresh herbs from their own gardens at home. 'We like it best to eat at home with our families and friends – we can create the simple Italian meals that we most enjoy in our own kitchens and appreciate them with the people that mean the most to us.' So that's why Magica Roma feels like a home from home.

Central Building,
8 Central Square,
Pinelands, Cape Town, 7405
+27 21 531 1489
GPS: S33°56'24.19"
E18°29'52.39"

Mediterranean platter – grilled Mediterranean-style vegetables topped with grilled baby calamari and moscardini

INGREDIENTS

eggplant
butternut
onions
a little oil
baby calamari tubes
moscardini
freshly chopped chilli and garlic, infused with olive oil
salt and pepper to taste
balsamic vinegar
olive oil

METHOD

Slice the eggplant, butternut and onions thinly and grill on a skillet with very little oil until browned. Grill the baby calamari tubes and moscardini until cooked, and season with chilli and garlic, salt and pepper. On a platter, lay out the thinly sliced vegetables and dress with balsamic vinegar and olive oil. Season to taste. Top the vegetables with the grilled calamari and moscardini and serve warm.

Restaurant Mosaic

an epicurean adventure inspired by nature, presented with excellence

"A must-do before you die."

The Orient,
Francolin Avenue,
Elandsfontein, Pretoria, 0001
+27 12 371 2902
www.restaurantmosaic.com
GPS: S25°45'40.49"
E27°59'56.77"

An escapade of pure indulgence awaits in the remote Francolin conservatory outside Pretoria at the Orient Boutique Hotel, where the Dartnell family have created an oasis for culinary pleasure. Previously a family farm, they have crafted what they call 'a restaurant with rooms'. Dad Dartnell is focused on the figures so that effervescent chef Chantel and her genuinely hospitable mom Mari can be playful and have fun. The family find time to travel for inspiration. Chantel does not eat out much, but loves both Tokara and Indochine when in the Cape.

You, too, may have to wait patiently on the approach road for a large tortoise or a zebra to move out of your way, giving you time to unwind in order to appreciate all on offer at what is known as 'the sanctuary of senses'. The hotel illustrates Moorish architecture and the restaurant is decorated in Chantel's favourite Parisian Belle Epoque era. Guests have been known to book one night in each of the suites in order to appreciate their version of the spice route. The Marrakesh royal suite (a dayroom, private balcony for breakfast and Moroccan-inspired bedroom and bathroom) will take your breath away. Attention to detail resonates in decor and extends into finer details such as appropriate reading matter.

Dinner will take your senses to new heights. Classical French cuisine is elevated to another level with a sense of theatre. Diminutive chef Chantel, always in attendance, welcomes each guest and explains the journey. When complimented on her level of innovation, she states, 'There are no new ideas – it is simply your interpretation. When you create something, an element of it has been seen before.' Every nuance of the evening will be etched in your senses, from the bread and butter to the last morsel. Presentation, both personal and plated, is of the utmost importance, from white-gloved silver service to edible trees that kick-start the show. There is botanical inspiration in all her dishes that create a symphony of sensory explosions from start to finish. Her favourites are the Alchemist's Infusion, as well as the Garden of Eden, which has more than 50 delicately plated components.

Take a morning walk on the guinea fowl trail or visit the Tienie Pritchard Museum, ideal for art lovers, before you tear yourself away for breakfast, which is sure to be another sensory adventure. Chantel's food, like Chantel, is playful, energetic and joyous. 'I love pretty.' Chantel is not just pretty. She is pretty amazing, and her food is commanding a new space in the South African culinary world. A must-do before you die.

INGREDIENTS

Beetroot meringues

4 raw beetroot
2 egg whites
125g icing sugar

Beetroot vinaigrette

1 large fresh beetroot, peeled and trimmed
1/2 cup olive oil
2 tablespoons red wine vinegar
1/2 teaspoon salt
1/4 teaspoon freshly ground pepper

Lemon vinaigrette

3 tablespoons fresh lime juice
zest of 1 lime
100ml lemon olive oil
coriander and basil leaves to taste
salt and pepper to taste

Gravlax

1kg yellowfin tuna fillet
1/2 cup Maldon salt
1 cup castor sugar
2 tablespoons freshly squeezed lime juice
1 tablespoon freshly ground pepper
1 stalk lemongrass, chopped
1 bunch fresh coriander, chopped
2 bunches fresh dill (don't skimp on the dill, as this is what gives gravlax its unique flavour)

METHOD

Beetroot meringues

Scrub and peel the beetroot. Boil for 30–60 minutes until cooked through (a fork should easily pierce the beetroot). Remove from liquid and cook the liquid down for another 45–60 minutes until it is reduced, thick and dark purple-red. To make the meringues, place the icing sugar and egg whites in a mixing bowl and whisk with an electric mixer until stiff peaks form, about five to eight minutes. Add as much of the beetroot syrup as required to get a rich dark purple-red colour in the meringue. Use a teaspoon to spoon meringue mixture onto a baking tray lined with greaseproof paper. Bake for 15–20 minutes at 160°C until crisp on the outside but not golden.

Beetroot vinaigrette

Cut beetroot into thin wedges and toss with one tablespoon of the olive oil. Place in a roasting pan. Bake at 200°C for 35 minutes or until tender. Cool for 15 minutes. Process the beetroot, the remaining olive oil, vinegar, salt and pepper in a food processor until smooth, stopping to scrape down the sides. Pour the mixture through a wire-mesh strainer into a bowl, discarding the solids.

Lemon vinaigrette

Place all the ingredients in a jug blender (or bar blender) and blitz, then pass the vinaigrette through a fine sieve and adjust the seasoning according to taste. The vinaigrette should have a sweet-sour taste and not be too overwhelming on the palate. To tone down acidity, add a bit of sugar, and to tone down on the harshness of the vinegar, add a bit more olive oil.

Gravlax

Place the tuna, skin side down, into a wide, shallow dish that fits the tuna snugly. Place the salt, sugar, lime juice and pepper into a clean bowl and mix well. Add the lemongrass and coriander and mix through. Spread the mixture over the tuna so that it is totally covered. Sprinkle the dill onto the paste-covered tuna and pat down. Press the dill onto the flesh. Turn the fish over in the dish so that the skin is facing upwards. Cover the dish with one layer of clingwrap. Press the clingwrap down onto the edges of the fish before wrapping it around the sides of the dish. Once this has been completed, repeat the process with another layer of clingwrap. Apply weight to the top of the fish to press it down into the dish (jars, tins or any other weights can be used). Transfer the fish to the fridge and leave for two to three days. After one day, unwrap the clingwrap from the dish and remove the tuna fillet. Brush off the herbs from the tuna, rewrap the tuna tightly in new clingwrap and place in the fridge until required. Place the tuna fillet on a carving board, flesh side up. With a long, sharp knife, carefully carve very thin diagonal slivers of the tuna – trim the sides up neatly so that the thin slices form a perfect square.

TO SERVE

Dip alternate slices of tuna in the beetroot vinaigrette and the lemon vinaigrette. Serve with cubed avocado topped with black sesame seeds, and beetroot meringues.

Chef's note: Gravlax is normally prepared using a salmon fillet with the skin on. It works equally well with a skinless fillet, or you can substitute any other fatty fish for the salmon if that is what is available at your local market.

Tuna and beetroot gravlax

Myoga

the theatre of the kitchen fused with the finest ingredients

60 Colinton Road,
Vineyard Hotel and Spa,
Newlands, 7700
+27 21 657 4545
www.myoga.co.za
GPS: S33°58'44.68"
E18°27'31.57"

The Vineyard Hotel in Newlands is a favourite with sports fans and also scores a hit with those wanting solace and natural beauty in this cooler part of Cape Town. The hotel and luxury spa are set in an idyllic six-acre garden where Lady Anne Barnard had her country house in the 1800s. Discerning diners are sure to be delighted with any of the restaurants at this hotel, but especially with their flagship Myoga, meaning 'ginger blossom' in Japanese. Their seven-course tasting menu is a marvellous illustration of the abilities of chef Mike Bassett. The new look is lighter and brighter than before, and all tables get a bird's-eye view of the open kitchen. Many fans of his former restaurant, Ginja, have come flocking to follow his innovation with food.

Mike's inspiration is a culmination of 20 years' experience, starting with training under Raymond Blanc of the Belmond Le Manoir aux Quat'Saisons, and the fun he has had in watching trends. He has developed quite a taste memory along with a reputation for superlative dining. His long-term staff enjoy learning from him. While the menu changes regularly, he is known to change a course at a time, so here nothing stands still. Elements of his cuisine come from the four corners of the globe, with strong, though not overpowering, Asian influences. There is umami in all his dishes - a combination of many flavours that work well together.

Mike's favourite food includes poultry and cheeseburgers and his favourite ingredient is scallops. He is ethical regarding ingredients, and has taken a stand against serving foie gras. His seven-course degustation menu is a surprise from start to finish. It is innovative, well harmonised and exceptional value. Service here is on a par with the excellent cuisine.

"Elements of his cuisine come from the four corners of the globe, with strong, though not overpowering, Asian influences."

INGREDIENTS

Avocado compound butter

200g ripe avocado
1 tablespoon freshly squeezed lemon juice
60g unsalted butter, softened
1 clove garlic, minced
1 tablespoon freshly chopped coriander leaves
2 teaspoons ground cumin
salt and freshly ground black pepper

Tortilla crumbs

1 1/3 cups unbleached all-purpose flour
2/3 cup yellow cornmeal (masa harina)
4 tablespoons cold-pressed grapeseed oil
1/2 cup water
1/2 teaspoon salt
1/4 teaspoon ancho chilli powder
1/4 teaspoon cumin
1/4 teaspoon onion powder
1/4 teaspoon garlic powder
1/4 teaspoon allspice

Ancho chilli prawns

16 medium prawns
1 tablespoon butter
1 tablespoon melted bone marrow
1 teaspoon ground ancho chilli
black salt to taste

Buffalo wings

8 chicken wings
1 tablespoon Mexican chilli paste in adobo
1 tablespoon butter
2 cloves garlic, crushed
1 tablespoon chicken stock
1 teaspoon tamari soy sauce
pinch of sea salt

Ranch spuma

1 cup crème fraîche
1/4 cup buttermilk
1/4 cup chopped fresh basil leaves
1/4 cup chopped fresh parsley leaves
2 tablespoons sliced fresh chives
1 teaspoon chopped fresh thyme leaves
1 clove garlic, chopped
juice of 1/2 lemon
1/4 teaspoon onion powder
1/3 cup crumbled blue cheese
sea salt and coarsely ground black pepper to taste
1 tablespoon cold proespuma (stabilises foams)

METHOD

Avocado compound butter

Peel and pit the avocado. Place all ingredients into the bowl of a food processor and process until well combined. Set in the fridge. When firm, make quenelles and set aside.

Tortilla crumbs

In a medium-sized bowl, mix the flour, cornmeal and oil. Gradually mix in the water and salt. Knead briefly, just until the dough is smooth.

Divide the dough into 10 pieces, weighing about 25g each. Roll the pieces into balls, flatten them slightly, and allow them to rest, covered, for at least 30 minutes. This resting period improves the texture of the dough by giving the flour time to absorb the water, and it also gives the gluten time to relax, making the tortillas easier to roll out.

Preheat a cast-iron griddle or heavy frying pan over medium heat. Working with one piece of dough at a time (keep the remaining dough balls covered), roll the balls out until they're about 10cm in diameter. Fry the tortillas in an ungreased pan for about 45 seconds on each side. Bake the tortillas in a hot oven until golden and crispy. When cool, crush them with the spices and season with some sea salt.

Ancho chilli prawns

Clean and devein the prawns and vac pack with the butter, melted bone marrow, ancho chilli and a pinch of black salt. Seal the vacuum pack and cook in a water bath at 55°C for 10 minutes. Remove the prawns from the bag and sauté in a hot frying pan for 30 seconds until just caramelised. Drain on kitchen towels and set aside until ready to serve.

Buffalo wings

Trim the chicken wings so that they resemble small drumsticks and place in a vac pack with the remaining ingredients. Seal the vac pack and cook in a sous-vide bath for one hour at 72°C. Remove from the vac pack and glaze in a hot frying pan until the sauce is thick and the wings are well coated. Set aside until ready to serve.

Ranch spuma

Place all the ingredients in a bowl, blend until smooth and strain. Place the strained dressing into a cream gun, charge with two cream bombs and leave in the fridge until required. There will always be a little left over for another time, or just divide the recipe in half.

Ancho chilli garlic chorizo prawns, mild buffalo wings, blue cheese ranch spuma, avocado butter, crushed tortilla

PLATING

Place the chicken wings, prawns and avocado butter neatly on a plate and release some of the ranch dressing from the cream gun onto the plate. Sprinkle with tortilla crumbs and serve.

Serves 4

Smoked salmon dish from Myoga

Nobu

2016/2017 Gourmet Guide

modern Japanese cuisine

One&Only Hotel,
Dock Road, V&A Waterfront,
Cape Town, 8001
+27 21 431 5111
www.noburestaurants.com
GPS: S33°54'30.95"
E18°24'59.22"

The One&Only Hotel is a major drawcard of the V&A Waterfront. Set on the waterway, it boasts a spa with its own lush, landscaped island plus spectacular views of the Mother City's mountain. Here you can eat at Reuben's or at the noted Nobu restaurant. Global icon Nobuyuki Matsuhisa's restaurants are legendary, and his Cape Town establishment is no exception to the rule.

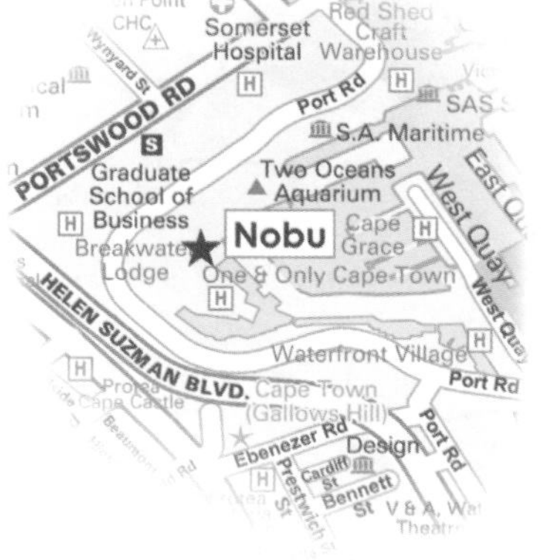

A trip to this chic double-volume restaurant is a treat, and not complete without tasting karate-loving chef Dil Tamang's signature dish of Alaskan black cod with miso sauce, which he marinates for three days before cooking in a salamander. Hailing from Nepal where he was born and schooled, it took him years of working his way through Kathmandu, experimenting with international cuisine, until he found himself in Dubai. He and his wife have been living in South Africa for two years, married in 2015. He was chef at Nobu in Dubai for three years, and took the opportunity to move here to learn about a country about which he previously knew nothing. The Tamangs like to cook Nepalese food – curry and fries – but also love pasta.

Dil's eyes light up when he talks about the sushi at Nobu, and he insists that the highlight is to take a seat at the counter to watch the masters in action, plus get sushi immediately at the right temperature, rather than waiting for it to be taken to a table. 'At Nobu our sushi is different from traditional sushi.' He won't eat sushi elsewhere, but loves relaxing in a nice place like Camps Bay for a meal.

If in doubt about what to order (other than the saké to drink, which is a must), take the easy option of a set menu or ask for expert advice. The staff at Nobu are enthusiastic, interesting and knowledgeable about the vast menu that embraces the best of Japanese flavours touched with South African and Indian spices. Nobu's Japanese cuisine is not truly typical – it is modern Japanese fused with South African influences. 'We call it innovative "New Style" Japanese cuisine. We use the freshest ingredients, prepared simply with a Japanese ethic and style. The flavours are a fusion of traditional Japanese with a Peruvian twist, and the result is dishes with layers of flavours that are presented deceptively simply but are simply great!'

It will take you to new heights in terms of innovative cuisine. 'People come to try my new things, and more people are getting to know about us. Regulars sometimes come for just their favourite dish. You have to have a reason for putting ingredients on a plate – colour as you look at your food first, secondly for taste and texture. Less is better.'

"The flavours are a fusion of traditional Japanese with a Peruvian twist, and the result is dishes with layers of flavours that are presented deceptively simply but are simply great!"

Chef Dil Tamang

Black cod den miso

INGREDIENTS

Dashi
3 litres water
6cm kombu (seaweed)
45g bonito flakes

Den miso
2.25 litres dashi (fish stock)
3.38kg sugar
1.13kg honey
3.75kg white miso paste

Yuzu miso
100g den miso
8g yuzu juice
8g rice vinegar

Black Cod
200g black cod
200ml den miso
50ml yuzu miso
hajikami (ginger) for garnishing

METHOD

Dashi
Boil the water with the kombu, then turn off the heat. Add the bonito flakes, leave to stand for 25 minutes and strain.

Den miso
Boil the dashi, add the sugar and honey and mix well. Stir in the miso paste and bring to the boil. Remove from heat to cool.

Yuzu miso
Mix all the ingredients.

Black cod
Cut a whole black cod into 200g pieces and marinate in den miso for 48-72 hours. Remove from the marinade and grill skin side down until skin is halfway burnt, then remove all the bones. Turn it over, add the yuzu miso on top of the black cod and cook in the oven for three minutes at 180-190°C. Place the cod under the grill to brown until golden. Garnish with hajikami.

ON19

contemporary cuisine that embraces the complexity of simplicity

Panoramic, sweeping views of the culture capital are not the only drawcard of The Westin Hotel adjacent to the CTICC in Cape Town. Whip your way up to the 19th floor and, after relaxing in the Heavenly Spa, treat your taste buds to a sumptuous meal at ON19 while retaining your commitment to health and wellbeing. It is more than the location that appeals to the busy traveller and those travelling for business. Here you will find an array of super foods, irresistible in spite of being good for you. Decor is simple, other than the dramatic geometric carpet, to avoid distraction from the breathtaking outlook.

Chef de Cuisine Anerith Smythe has worked under food icons in exotic destinations like Dubai, Kuwait and the Maldives, returning to South Africa to join The Westin. Her philosophy is that food should be enjoyed, using only the freshest of produce prepared in simplistic ways to enhance their natural flavours. She also believes that food should be balanced and healthy. Her inspiration comes from the surrounding environment and fresh produce. 'It also comes from my family, the way we always spend time around the table during meals, talking and enjoying ourselves. Food, to me, brings people together.'

Anerith favours fresh, good quality fruits and vegetables, and likes a variety of cuisines from all over the world, especially Thai cuisine.

The menu at ON19 changes seasonally. 'I believe in cooking with the seasons to enjoy produce that is fresh, flavourful, at its best, readily available and at the lowest cost. Sustainability is important to me and I try to use produce that is grown and/or raised in an ethically/organically responsible way at all times. This includes food production as well.'

The Westin Hotel,
Cape Town Convention Square,
Lower Long Street, Cape Town
+27 21 412 9999
www.on19restaurant.co.za
GPS: S33°54'55.24"
E18°25'33.19"

INGREDIENTS

160g baby new potatoes
20g shallots, finely chopped
20ml white wine vinegar
80g fennel bulbs
6 orange segments
4 lemon segments
salt and pepper to taste
250ml orange juice
10ml sugar
2 x 155g salmon fillets (skin on)
salt
15ml extra virgin olive oil

METHOD

Boil the potatoes until cooked, but not too soft. Once cooled, cut into quarters. Finely chop shallots and sauté in a frying pan. Add potatoes and white wine vinegar. Cook until the vinegar has evaporated.

For the salad, thinly slice the fennel bulbs, add the orange and lemon segments and season with salt and pepper.

For the orange reduction, place the orange juice and sugar in a small saucepan over medium heat to dissolve the sugar. Then reduce the liquid by half.

Season the salmon with salt and drizzle with 5ml of the olive oil. Heat the remaining oil in a frying pan over medium heat. Once the pan is hot enough, place the salmon in the hot oil, skin side down. Cook until skin is crispy (about two minutes) and turn over. Cook salmon until the desired temperature.

PLATING

Place the potatoes in the centre of the plate, the salmon on top of the potatoes and arrange the salad on top of the salmon. Lastly, drizzle orange reduction over the salmon and enjoy.
Serves 2

Pan-fried salmon with shallot potatoes, fennel salad and orange reduction

oneNINEone at the Hyatt

modern African gastronomy

One could be anywhere in the world when one steps into the revamped Hyatt Hotel. It's a cosmopolitan space and The Lobby Lounge has always been a meeting hot spot.

The restaurant has gone through many changes over the past 20 years and now opens onto a lush garden terrace. The decor has an up-market feel, with its double-volume space and combination of textures. Chefs are on display in cleverly designed open-plan kitchens, and a novelty is the plating island where chefs finish their dishes – all part of the theatre of the meal. 'oneNINEone is a show kitchen restaurant where guests are treated to an up-market food offering in an unpretentious setting; a place where we cater for most palates,' says Executive Chef Andrew Atkinson.

The wine list is extensive, with more than 170 local and international bottles on the menu. The dinner menu is seasonal and small – only seven starters, seven mains and five desserts – but with a focus on edgy, innovative flavours combined with classical cooking styles. Expect popular grills like rib eye steak, lamb cutlets and wagyu beef fillet, and innovative combinations such as black salt sea bass served with grilled peaches.

Executive sous chef Shaneil Dinna is very hands-on and his philosophy is to use sustainable, seasonal ingredients. Vegetables play a big part of each dish and are not just treated as a side dish. The menu changes with the seasons and is kept light with fresh local ingredients. It reflects influences from South Africa's entire cultural heritage, namely African, French, German, British, Indian and Asian.

'The food is not fussy, complicated or pretentious. It is simple and attractive, enhancing the natural flavours and colours of the ingredients. We aim to impress our guests with our unique combinations and our sincere service.'

Hyatt Hotel, 191 Oxford Road,
Rosebank, Johannesburg, 2132
+27 11 280 1234
http://johannesburg.regency.hyatt.com/en/hotel/dining/oneNINEone-restaurant.html
GPS: S26°08'37.15"
E28°02'35.60"

"...a novelty is the plating island where chefs finish their dishes – all part of the theatre of the meal."

oneNINEone's dining room

Orinoco

17 Bree Street,
Cape Town, 8001
+27 21 418 4544
http://orinocoflavours.co.za
GPS: S33°55'04.93"
E18°25'18.61"

traditional and modern Latino cuisine with a touch of fusion

At the bottom of the culinary block in Bree Street sits the little cornucopia of flavours called Orinoco. Daytime clientele come from office blocks nearby for the daily specials, with favourites such as the tacos, burritos and quesadillas. By night there is a more relaxed ambience when those in the know arrive for the extensive evening tapas menu.

Venezuelan Migdalia Bellorin hails from the exotic island of Margherita. Her inspiration comes from her Latin American roots, Venezuela where she was born and Mexico where she lived for five years while undergoing formal chef training. 'My cooking instruction began at my grandmother's apron strings and she more than anyone taught me the joy of bringing happiness to others through food. My extensive travels in Latin America have exposed me to a wide variety of culinary styles and dishes, from simple village food in the high Andes to the sophisticated inventions of the new breed of gourmet chefs in Mexico City and Lima. I love it all and my menus reflect this wonderful range of culinary delights.'

There is even a Japanese influence in the food, like the fish tacos, with a combination of Mexican chilli and teriyaki sauce. They aim to be seasonal and sustainable, avoiding endangered fish species such as kingklip. Instead, Migdalia uses excellent alternatives such as silvers, angelfish and yellowtail for her renowned specialities like ceviche. She likes the bold flavours that come from fresh herbs, spice seasonings and, of course, chillies. 'Used well, these can bring great taste to relatively mundane basic ingredients such as our hand-made corn tortillas and all types of meat, fish and vegetables. Sauces, garnishes and presentation are indispensable to my culinary style, so there are always fresh avocados, micro herbs, soft cheeses and lightly pickled vegetables in my kitchen.'

Venezuelans and Colombians name the arepa as their favourite street food or snack – a grilled cornmeal flatbread that can be filled with just about anything. 'I love rustic soups such as the Venezuelan sancocho, which is prepared many ways, usually to a traditional family recipe – a mixture of different meats and vegetables (including corn cobs) cooked in a huge pot, often for family picnics. Above all, I enjoy Mexican dishes and the Tacos de Cochinita pibil presented here are a great favourite of mine.'

Migdalia also loves pasta, especially at A Tavola, and Franck Dangereux's Foodbarn.

INGREDIENTS

Venezuelan guasacaca green sauce

300g fresh coriander
300g fresh parsley
1 small green chilli
pinch of salt
dash of vinegar to taste

Pork and tortillas

½ leg or shoulder of pork
1 red onion, peeled and chopped
2-3 carrots, cut into pieces
2-3 cloves garlic, whole
1 aji (green or red chilli), to taste
1 bay leaf
3 cloves
1 stick cinnamon
1 teaspoon cumin seeds
sufficient orange juice to cover the above ingredients
250ml (1 cup) lime juice, sufficient just to cover the pork
salt to taste
20 small corn tortillas, or wheat wraps if tortillas are not available
micro herbs or alfalfa for garnish
handful fresh coriander leaves
15ml (1 tablespoon) Venezuelan guasacaca green sauce and/or guacamole

METHOD

Venezuelan guasacaca green sauce

Blend together all the ingredients for the sauce.

Pork and tortillas

Place the pork, vegetables and aromatics in an ovenproof dish or pot. Cover these with the orange and lime juice and bring gently to the boil on the stove. Cover the dish or pot and transfer to the oven, heated to 180°C, and cook for at least two hours. Remove from the oven and check the pork – it should be soft and moist. Continue cooking if the meat is still firm, but do not allow to dry. When cooked, set aside the pork and strain off the vegetables and spices. Reserve the cooking liquid. Shred the pork with a spoon and fork and add some of the cooking juices if more moisture is required, but not the point where the mix becomes runny. Season with salt to taste.

Heat the tortillas on a dry hot plate and heap a tablespoon of the meat onto each one. Garnish with micro herbs and a few fresh coriander leaves. Serve hot with small bowls of guasacaca and/or guacamole on the side. Guests can top with the sauces and roll or fold the tacos by hand ready to eat.

Tacos de Cochinita Pibil

Overture

modern, fresh and local South African cuisine

Hidden Valley Wines,
Annandale Road,
Stellenbosch, 7600
+27 21 880 2721
www.dineatoverture.co.za
GPS: S34°00'03.46"
E18°50'22.41"

"His food is contemporary and complex, yet clean and uncontrived, distinctively flavoured and perfectly plated."

There are many reasons to visit Hidden Valley wine estate in Stellenbosch. It could be for a wine tasting, an olive tasting, a chocolate and wine pairing, to sample their wines with a cheese and charcuterie platter, or simply to laze in nature and enjoy a leisurely picnic with sweeping vineyard views. Whatever the reason, make sure that lunch at Overture is top of your list. This restaurant is where loudly lauded (with good reason) chef Bertus Basson delights diners with new takes on old flavours using only the finest ingredients.

The breathtaking views of the surrounding terroir are as good as the vista of the master at work in the kitchen. His food is contemporary and complex, yet clean and uncontrived, distinctively flavoured and perfectly plated. The menu at Overture is in continuous evolution as Bertus is constantly innovating. Marry your meal with wines from Hidden Valley or other local and international wines.

He gets his inspiration from old South African family recipes. He loves any ingredient that is fresh and local, and cheerfully admits to having a bit of a vegetable fetish. 'I love impala tartar. It's a homage to hunting with my father when I was a kid.' Bertus's approach to seasonality and sustainability is simple: 'All of our food is seasonal; you won't find a strawberry here in winter. We try to serve only food from sustainable and renewable resources.'

He likes to eat at Rust en Vrede for a special occasion, and for a casual meal chooses Genki or Schoon de Companje in Stellenbosch. South China Dim Sum Bar in Long Street, Cape Town, is also a favourite.

Bertus is also pulling the crowds at his more recently opened restaurant at Spice Route, where there is a smorgasbord of gastro opportunities, yet he stands, once again, head and shoulders above the crowd.

INGREDIENTS

Brine

1 packet brine mix
12 litres water
2 heads garlic, split
15 cloves
15 black peppercorns
20 coriander seeds

Pork bellies

6 pork bellies
20 litres water
1 litre soy sauce
5 star anise
100g whole ginger

Shallots and carrots

2kg peeled shallots
2kg peeled carrots, split and halved
100ml oil
salt to taste

Pears

15 pears, halved
400g sugar
3 tablespoons ground cinnamon
salt to taste
300ml oil

Carrot purée

1kg carrots, peeled and chopped
200g onions, sliced
20g whole garlic
5g thyme
100g butter
20g salt

METHOD

Brine

Dissolve the brine mix in the water, and add the garlic and spices.

Pork bellies

Brine the pork bellies for 24 hours. Bring the water, soy sauce, star anise and ginger to a simmer, add the brined bellies and simmer for two hours. Remove the bellies and press. Skim and reduce the cooking stock by half. Reserve this as the sauce.

Shallots and carrots

Coat the shallots and carrots with oil and season to taste. Place in an oven tray and roast in the oven at 120°C for about 20 minutes or until vegetables are soft.

Pears

Toss all of the ingredients together and place in an oven tray. Cover with tinfoil and roast until soft and tender.

Carrot purée

Steam all the ingredients together for one hour and 20 minutes. Strain and blend until very smooth.

TO SERVE

Crisp a portion of belly on the grill. Heat some of the braising liquid. Heat a portion of shallots and carrots, and a pear. Heat the purée. Serve in a bowl plate. Flood with braising liquid.

Pork belly with carrot purée, carrots and pears

Planet Restaurant

pure culinary artistry on a plate

76 Orange Street,
Gardens, Cape Town, 8001
+27 21 483 1948
www.belmond.com/
mount-nelson-hotel-cape-town/
planet_restaurant
GPS: S33°55'52.70"
E18°24'47.69"

For more than a century, the landmark Belmond Mount Nelson has guaranteed opulence and grace – an oasis from the hustle and bustle of Cape Town city. Here olde-worlde grace and charm gently collide with what is now.

The Planet Restaurant offers formal fine dining with sophistication. Start with drinks at the popular Planet Bar, and do some celeb-spotting before moving through to the restaurant. The best way to sample the stellar food of executive chef Rudi Liebenberg is at his Chef's Table. A maximum of 16 guests eat in the kitchen, savour his innovative cuisine and glean gourmet tips from this maestro.

Rudi is known for innovative twists on old favourites, for versatility and passion that concentrate on sourcing the best (local) produce. 'It's all about the ingredients and nature. My job is to enhance perfection, to do as little as possible to perfect ingredients. Seasonal means using ingredients at their prime. I have made a commitment to myself – to have integrity as a chef and to be honest about what I put on a plate.' Rudi's artistry (he starts the planning of each plate with a sketch) and the Nellie's famous high tea draw visitors from far and wide.

If you are looking for Rudi you may also find him dining at Chefs Warehouse & Canteen, Jordan, Overgaauw, South China Dim Sum Bar or the Woodlands Eatery.

INGREDIENTS

Roast chicken

1 whole chicken, breast left on crown and trimmed
2 drumsticks, wings and thighs on the bone
black pepper
coarse salt
butter and oil as needed
1 chilli
3 cloves garlic, lightly crushed, still in skin
2 cloves
1 sprig thyme
mirepoix vegetables, rough cut
  2 carrots
  1 onion
  1 celery stick
250ml chicken stock
250ml red wine

Roast chicken filling

250g roasted chicken
$^1/_4$ teaspoon lemon zest
2 teaspoons chopped parsley
1 small chilli (from roasting pan)
3 cloves garlic (from roasting pan)
35g chopped walnuts
$^1/_2$ onion, roasted in skin for 45 minutes, then chopped
80g feta cheese
1 tablespoon grated Parmesan cheese
salt and black pepper
1 tablespoon chopped chives

Enriched pasta dough for tortelloni

500g white cake flour
1 teaspoon salt
4 eggs
3 egg yolks
1 tablespoon olive oil

Cauliflower purée and roasted cauliflower florets

700g cauliflower
salt and pepper to taste
100g butter
2 cloves garlic
110ml cream
$^1/_2$ onion, roasted in skin for 45 minutes

Final assembly and plating

150g roasted cauliflower florets
200g cauliflower purée
100ml jus
30g butter
salt and coarse black pepper
2 sprigs thyme
2 chicken breasts, cooked and removed from crown
30–40g young spinach
20–25 chicken tortelloni, blanched
60g butter
10–15 sage leaves
30g Parmesan shavings

METHOD

Roast chicken

Season the chicken. Warm an oven-proof roasting dish on stove and add one tablespoon oil and two tablespoons butter. Place chicken in dish with split chilli, garlic, cloves and thyme and brown evenly. Add vegetables and continue cooking without burning. Dot with butter. Deglaze with two tablespoons of stock. Place in moderate oven for about 20 minutes. Remove crown, and continue cooking thighs and drumsticks until cooked through – about 30 minutes. Allow to rest and cool, then remove breast from the crown. Separate meat, bones and skin. Chop removed meat and skin. Cut bones and crown smaller and place back in the pan with the juices. Deglaze the jus with red wine and add remaining chicken stock. Cook for 30 minutes and strain. Adjust seasoning, and set aside until needed.

Roast chicken filling

Chop the deboned roasted chicken into very small cubes with skin. Add the lemon zest, parsley, chilli and garlic from roasting pan, walnuts, onion, feta and Parmesan. Add some of the remaining roasting liquid to moisten. Adjust the seasoning and add the chives. Mix to combine. Make 25–30 equal-sized balls of filling (approximately 12g per ball).

Enriched pasta dough for tortelloni

Place all of the ingredients into a food processor, and combine. Turn the dough out and knead for about three to four minutes. Wrap in clingwrap and rest in a cool place for at least 30 minutes. Unwrap the dough and press it out by hand as thinly as possible, in order to fit into the pasta machine. Roll the pasta through the machine, continuously adjusting the setting to be thinner and thinner. Roll the pasta to a thickness of approximately 1mm.

To make the tortelloni

Place a sheet of pasta dough onto a floured surface. (You could use semolina for this.) Cut into rounds of 7–8cm in diameter. Place filling onto the centre of each round. Fold the pasta over the filling so that it resembles a half moon and squeeze edges to seal. Take the two ends and bring them together, overlapping slightly – not by the easiest route, but rather horizontally across, folding the thickest part around your finger and bringing the ends together. Squeeze and place onto a floured surface.

Fill a large saucepan with salted water and bring to the boil. Cook tortelloni for a few minutes until al dente. Refresh in ice water if you are not going to use immediately.

Cauliflower purée and roasted cauliflower florets
Cut 150g of neat florets from the cauliflower head and season. In a non-stick pan, sauté the florets with 60g of the butter until crisp and light brown; finish in oven if needed.

Cut the remainder of the cauliflower into chunks, season and cover with tinfoil. Roast in a preheated oven at 180°C with garlic, cream and the remaining 40g butter. Continue to roast until soft – this will take about 30 minutes. Remove tinfoil and continue to roast for a further 15 minutes. Take care not to burn the mix – stir and turn all the time until it starts to caramelise.

Place in a blender. Add the cooking liquid as needed, as well as the roasted onion, and blend the mixture to a smooth purée. Adjust seasoning as needed.

FINAL ASSEMBLY AND PLATING
Heat roasted cauliflower, heat purée, heat jus.

Place butter in a heated pan with pepper, thyme and chicken breasts. Gently finish cooking, dotting with butter and seasoning as needed. Add spinach and allow to wilt. Set aside to rest.

Fill a large saucepan with salted water and bring to the boil. Reheat the tortelloni and place straight into a non-stick saucepan with slightly burnt butter and sage. Season and set aside.

Cut chicken breasts lengthways. Place purée on plate, place chicken on top of purée, arrange cauliflower and tortelloni on plate with spinach, add jus, and finish with some Parmesan shavings.
Serves 4

Roast chicken tortelloni

The Pot Luck Club

petite plates, perfect impressions at a gourmet playground

"He cleverly conjures up flavour and visual combinations with perfect appeal..."

Head for the Old Biscuit Mill in the Woodstock precinct, venture six stories up in a glass lift (to the top of the silo) and land in culinary heaven. Topped with the most glorious 360° view of a vibey city, The Pot Luck Club is where luminary chef Luke Dale-Roberts experiments and plays alongside his internationally acclaimed Test Kitchen. 'I enjoy opening a restaurant as much as I enjoy my craft.' The Saxon in Joburg is the latest spot for his fans.

Choose a seat at the counter for up close and personal, or take a table to relax and work your way through a menu that is divided into five flavours – sweet, salty, sour, bitter and umami – with a sweet endings selection. Tick off on an order sheet what takes your fancy, and your delectable plates, to share, will be slickly served. If undecided and you see it on the menu, ask for the celeriac salad, the famous fish sliders and the pork belly. Lunch is followed by two dinner sittings. Sunday brunches with bubbles and Bloody Marys are also the talk of the town.

Dale-Roberts' savvy business instinct is married with exceptional gourmet expertise and a genuine will to please. Here the discerning diner appreciates more accessible food and simpler platings than at The Test Kitchen. The ever-evolving menu allows Luke to explore his creative genius using fresh produce on his doorstep. He cleverly conjures up flavour and visual combinations with perfect appeal – a fusion of classic and quirky with strong Asian innovation. Head chef Wesley Randles has been there since opening.

Small portions, big scope – ideal for the astute, experimental diner.

6, The Silo,
The Old Biscuit Mill,
373–375 Albert Road,
Woodstock, Cape Town, 7925
+27 21 447 0804
http://thepotluckclub.co.za
GPS: S33°55'39.93"
E18°27'27.45"

INGREDIENTS

Honey mustard dressing

2 1/2 tablespoons honey
2 1/2 tablespoons Dijon mustard
150ml white wine vinegar
salt
375ml vegetable oil
2 1/2 tablespoons wholegrain mustard

Blue cheese cream

300ml cream
100g blue cheese

Broccoli

250g tenderstem broccoli
olive oil
Maldon salt
40g toasted walnuts, chopped
40g toasted flaked almonds

METHOD

Light a fire and allow to burn until the flames die and the coals are hot. Clean the broccoli stems and set aside until use.

Honey mustard dressing

Place the honey, Dijon mustard, white wine vinegar and pinch of salt into a blender. While the blender is running, slowly add the oil to emulsify the dressing. Season with another pinch of salt if required and stir in the wholegrain mustard at the end.

Blue cheese cream

Heat the cream, melt in the blue cheese and use a stick blender to emulsify the sauce. Reduce the sauce to a thick consistency.

Broccoli

Dress the broccoli stems with olive oil and season with Maldon salt. Place them on a grid over the fire. Cook for about two minutes until they are golden on the one side. Turn the broccoli and cook for another two minutes. Place the BBQ broccoli into a bowl, lightly dress it with the honey mustard dressing and chopped walnuts.

PLATING

Place a 20ml ladle of the blue cheese sauce into each serving bowl. Plate the broccoli in each bowl with the heads in the sauce and the stem sticking up. Finish off with a sprinkle of toasted almonds and a drizzle of olive oil.
Serves 4-6

BBQ broccoli with blue cheese

THE POT
LUCK CLUB

Punchinello's

a Venetian twist

Southern Sun Montecasino,
Montecasino Boulevard,
Johannesburg, 2055
+27 11 367 4367
www.tsogosun.com/punchinellos
GPS: S26°01'27.44" E28°00'47.22"

The hotel setting is opulent without being over the top. Crystal chandeliers and rich colours are toned down a notch by the bustling, open-plan kitchen showing chefs at work. It's a lively atmosphere with an air of professionalism in the service and presentation. This could be thanks to Punchinello's monthly 'Chefs of Distinction' dinners, where celebrated guest chefs are invited to cook in the kitchen.

The Venetian food theme ties in with Montecasino's traditional Italian design, and even local favourites on the menu have a twist. Grilled meat is also Venetian in cooking style so the addition of steaks to the menu is not far off the mark. Chargrilled veggie smears and purées add a gourmet element to your plate.

Executive chef Jade Sullaphen's philosophy is to keep the food simple but with a sustainable focus on seasonal ingredients. The offering is quite meaty, including the popular Daily Steak Specials, pork belly, lamb shank and chicken options – all served with polenta or pasta. There are a few pasta dishes in addition to three seafood choices. A big drawcard is the Mediterranean Table, a buffet-style medley of mezze, antipasti, tapas and baked breads. 'We believe in handling food with respect and finesse, and our attention to detail shows our passion for each ingredient.'

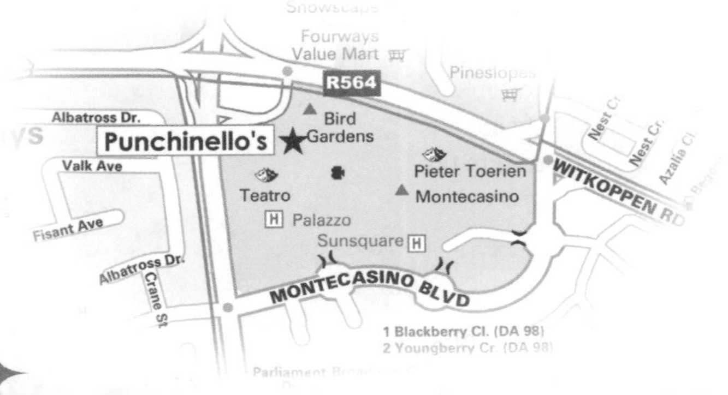

Chicken and mushroom ballotine

INGREDIENTS

180g chicken breast fillets
salt and pepper to taste
30g button mushrooms
30g each white and brown shimeji mushrooms
25g butter
1 egg
25ml cream
10g white onion, peeled
5g red onion, peeled
10g cherry tomato
5ml olive oil
2g micro greens

METHOD

Flatten a large chicken breast and season with salt and pepper. In a blender, blend another chicken breast to a smooth paste. Sauté the button mushrooms and some of the shimeji mushrooms with the butter in a pan. Add the mushrooms, egg and cream to the chicken pâté and season. Spoon the chicken pâté onto the centre of the flattened chicken fillet and form a roulade. Roll in clingwrap and steam to hold its shape. Place in the fridge to firm up.

Make a salsa by chopping the onions and cherry tomato into small cubes. Season to taste.

Layer some of the salsa onto a plate and slice the chicken ballotine onto the salsa. Drizzle with more of the salsa and the olive oil, scatter micro greens and the remaining shimeji mushrooms on top and serve.
Serves 1

Quentin at Oakhurst

contemporary Cape country cooking

Dorman Way, Hout Bay,
Cape Town, 7806
+27 21 790 4888
www.oakhurstbarn.com/the-restaurant.aspx
GPS: S34°01'08.42"
E18°22'35.00"

The provenance of the Oakhurst Farm in Hout Bay lends itself well to the ethos and experience of chef Quentin Spickernell's cuisine. By day, feel the crunch of the acorns underfoot and the shade of the old oak tree above on the patio and terrace; by night, enjoy the gleaming glamour of the chandeliers and refined white linen. Here the seasonal bounty is transformed into comfort foods during winter or seen simply served at its best in summer. There is an original wine cellar that has a good selection of local wines to match your choice of food.

Quentin's cooking background spanned many exotic locations, and he has been lauded for cooking for the rich and famous, having been responsible for Sol Kerzner's noteworthy New Year parties nearby for many years. Now he chooses to honour the soil and stay close to the sea, serving simple and sumptuous, robust and rustic 'un-fatigued' food. 'I am a strict convert to seasonal eating. Nothing beats the anticipation of the first asparagus crop. Sustainability is a guiding principle, although not without its own unintended consequences.' Parts of his menu change weekly, others twice a year. His favourite dish is a curry, and his choice ingredients are whole Cape seed spices.

Quentin has no special preferences for special-occasion dining, but if you want to know where to find him eating his favourite casual meal, it will be at 'Kalky's' in Hout Bay Harbour.

INGREDIENTS

1 small bushel thyme or lemon thyme, leaves stripped from stem
1 teaspoon cracked fennel seeds (optional)
1 sprig fresh parsley
zest and juice of 1 large lemon
100g hazelnuts, plus extra for garnishing
4 slices bread, blended to crumbs
salt and freshly ground black pepper
4 x 250–280g portions sustainable white linefish, skinned and deboned
1 handful rosa tomatoes, halved
olive oil, to sear
2 handfuls baby English spinach
30g butter

METHOD

Preheat the oven to 170°C. Coarsely chop the thyme, fennel seeds (if using), parsley, lemon zest and hazelnuts, and combine these ingredients with the breadcrumbs by hand. Season to taste.

Pat the fish fillets dry, then loosely pack the crumble onto the fish. Do not pat it down. Roast the fish in the oven for 12–15 minutes, depending on the thickness of the portions. Remove from oven.

In a frying pan over high heat, sear the tomatoes in a little olive oil. Add the spinach and allow it to wilt down. Season with salt and pepper.

Remove the fish from the roasting pan, drop in the butter and allow to melt for about a minute. Add the lemon juice and swirl, scraping the pan residue into the sauce.

To serve, place some spinach and tomato mix on each plate. Top with the fish and sprinkle the lemon butter around it. (Do not pour the juices over the fish as the crumble will become soggy.) Garnish with hazelnuts.
Serves 4

Quentin's crusted linefish

"...the seasonal bounty is transformed into comfort foods during winter or seen simply served at its best in summer."

Qunu

classic flavours combined with innovation and the unexpected

"Werner Snoek's food is nothing short of absolutely heavenly."

The Saxon Hotel,
36 Saxon Road, Sandhurst,
Johannesburg, 2196
+27 11 292 6000
www.saxon.co.za/qunu.html
GPS: S26°06'41.26"
E28°02'06.93"

The Saxon Hotel, the ultimate in luxury and privacy, has a legacy of award-winning chefs. This five-star urban sanctuary hotel with spa has always been synonymous with innovation and top-class, cutting-edge cuisine. After Rudi Liebenberg and David Higgs, Qunu keeps the culinary flag flying. Every effort is made for guests to feel special and cocooned from the hustle and bustle of nearby Sandton. Saxon staff treat business tycoons, state presidents and the man on the street to the same flawless hospitality, showing an innate pride in being part of this property. The African decor has been brightened by bursts of robust red, and the live sounds of the tinkling piano and the sexy sax add a special touch.

The service at Qunu is discreet yet attentive, informative but not over-whelming, Werner Snoek's food is nothing short of absolutely heavenly. Be sure to order his 'Taste of Africa', which allows him to say 'this is me' and reminisce about time spent in Mozambique. It is beer-braised oxtail with biltong chima, spinach matapa and chakalaka, or choose his deconstructed bouillabaisse. He likes doing traditional differently, giving a modern take to old classics. His sweet potato brûlée is a good example. This young and energetic chef is heartened by seeing the restaurant full, and getting good feedback since its rejuvenation. The experienced sommelier will lead you through their extensive wine list of local and imported labels.

If you are lucky enough to stay in one of the villas, you will wake to the sounds of birds on your private terrace and take the long walk along the undulating elevated wooden pathway back to the main hotel, echoing the surprises on Qunu's menu – what Werner calls his 'twists and turns'.

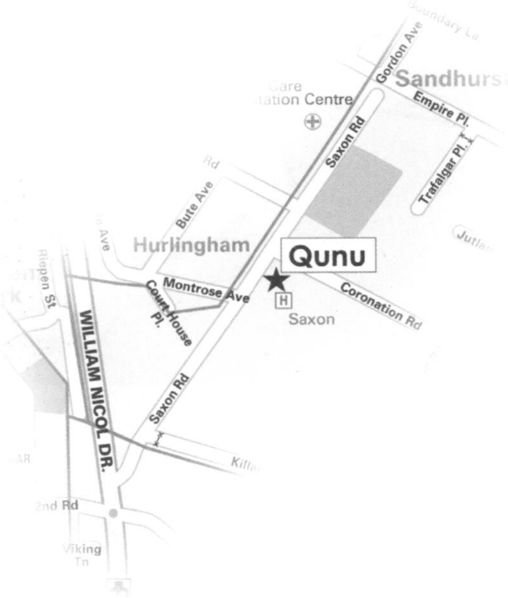

Karan beef fillet, wild mushroom ragoût, mashed potato, steamed baby vegetables, flambéed at your table and served with brandy mushroom sauce.

INGREDIENTS

Brandy mushroom sauce

50g butter
2 cloves garlic, crushed
3 spring onions, crushed
100g button mushrooms, sliced
1 tablespoon brandy
1 cup cream

METHOD

Brandy mushroom sauce

Melt the butter in frying pan over moderate heat and add the garlic, spring onions and mushrooms. Cook until mushrooms are golden brown. Add the brandy and cream and bring to the boil. Turn down heat and simmer for five minutes or until the sauce has thickened. Serve poured over the steak.

"He likes doing traditional differently, giving a modern take to old classics."

Red Chamber

Chinese food for sharing

Shop No. 68 U, Hyde Park Corner Shopping Centre, Corner of Jan Smuts Avenue and 6th Road, Sandton, 2196
+27 11 325 6048
www.redchamber.co.za
GPS: S26°07'34.35" E28°02'00.88"

Red Chamber owner, Emma Chen, opened her restaurant 26 years ago and her Chinese heritage is still her passion. The revamped restaurant in Hyde Park Shopping Centre is more contemporary. The new façade is inviting and the decor is inspired – an inside mirrored wall, representing water, meets a panel of oversized green bamboo prints.

The menu has evolved – from set menus, where diners could experience multiple courses, to strictly à la carte. She's added more authentic dishes to the menu and dares not take anything off the menu. The offering is extensive, plus there's an ample wine list designed to 'excite the flavours of our dishes'.

The restaurant has a no-MSG policy, uses no butter or cheese, and there's a 'health corner' on the menu. As a healthy option, don't miss the spicy cucumber salad – a simple mix of sweet-and-sour cucumber with chilli. It's the perfect choice to cleanse your palate.

Expect spicy dishes as Mandarin food is fiery, with ingredients like Szechuan peppercorn, dry chilli and sesame oil. If you're brave, try the fire cracker beef. The half Peking duck and shrimp salad served with lettuce 'cups' is a great combo for two to share. The tactile act of wrapping and rolling your meal is all part of the dining experience, and it's a taste sensation. Chopsticks add to the fun.

'Chinese food is not about one dish – it's all about variety. My challenge is to convince people to share dishes.'

The view from The Restaurant at Waterkloof

The Restaurant at Waterkloof

elevating classic fine dining to contemporary excellence

The Restaurant at Waterkloof in Somerset West has enviable views. This modern 120-seater restaurant perches over vineyards in a breathtaking glass promontory to maximise them. Here chef Greg Czarnecki has become renowned for his classic yet modern French cuisine. The open kitchen allows guests to watch him create his dishes. The decor is stylish and elegant, yet unpretentious, relying on the distracting views and sunsets in summer, roasting fires in winter.

Waterkloof Wine Estate,
Sir Lowry's Pass Village Street,
Somerset West, 7130
+27 21 858 1491
www.waterkloofwines.co.za
GPS: S34°06'29.25"
E18°52'47.97"

The popular two- and three-course and degustation menus are seasonal, and well married with Waterkloof wines. In crafting his dishes, this chef illustrates the same sensitive intelligence required by the biodynamic farming exercised on Waterkloof. Some dishes can come and go as certain products are only available for a short period of time. 'It is very important to be sustainable. We are looking at our own future. And even though we cook on a small scale with our restaurants, together we can make a change and also educate the staff and the customer to make the right choice.' His choice of a restaurant, if given a flight, would be Mosaic at the Orient. For a casual meal he chooses Genki Sushi in Stellenbosch.

"Inspiration can come from anywhere: a season, a product, someone, something you ate."

CHEF GREG CZARNECKI

Regulars select his Norwegian salmon gravlax and the oven-roasted aubergine and masala for starters. For mains, the Mauritian sea bass with Saldanha mussels and the Karoo braised lamb shoulder tick all the boxes.

Greg favours free-range and farm-fresh, liking earthy ingredients and cooking with the 'forgotten' vegetables that don't always attract – turnip, cabbage, celeriac and parsley root. He finds it difficult to pinpoint a signature dish, but currently recommends the foie gras with hibiscus. 'Inspiration can come from anywhere: a season, a product, someone, something you ate. It's actually fascinating how the creative process comes alive in your head.'

And creative he is. He describes his cuisine as contemporary with a modern twist. Others say exceptional.

Oven-roasted aubergine and masala

INGREDIENTS

Aubergine

60ml olive oil
2 tablespoons masala spice
3 large exotic aubergines
30ml cooking oil
salt and pepper to taste

Crispy aubergine skins

skins from 3 aubergines
1 teaspoon cornflour
salt to taste

Aubergine caviar

1 exotic aubergine
2 tablespoons mascarpone
salt and pepper to taste

Soft goat's cheese and milk gel

400ml milk
1 teaspoon agar agar
200g goat's cheese
salt and pepper to taste

Masala buttermilk

a little olive oil
1 small onion, finely chopped
1 shallot, finely chopped
1 clove garlic, crushed
5 sprigs thyme
1 small bay leaf
1 tablespoon masala spice
500ml buttermilk

Masala foam

400ml cream
1 medium onion, finely chopped
1 shallot, finely chopped
1 clove garlic, crushed
5 sprigs thyme
1 small bay leaf
2 tablespoons masala spice
400ml chicken stock
2 teaspoons lecithin

Masala nuts

100g hazelnuts
2 tablespoons masala spice

METHOD

Aubergine

Mix the olive oil with the masala spice. Peel the aubergines and reserve the skins. Rub the masala oil mix on the aubergines to cover the surface. Heat the cooking oil in a frying pan to the maximum temperature. Add the aubergines and rotate slowly until they are completely charred, creating a nice black bark coating. Remove them from the pan and place on a draining rack in the fridge to cool down. Cut two of the aubergines lengthways into four pieces, then remove the top and the tail by cutting each one off diagonally. Place them in a small roasting dish and season with salt and pepper, ready to heat them later.

Crispy aubergine skins

Julienne the skins. Coat them in cornflour and deep-fry at 100°C for one or two minutes until crispy. Remove the skins from the oil and place them on a tray with paper towels to drain the excess oil. Season with salt.

Aubergine caviar

Place the leftover aubergine in the oven at 200°C for 15-30 minutes until thoroughly cooked. Using a blender, make a smooth purée. Add the mascarpone and season with salt and pepper. Pass the purée through a sieve for a smoother result.

Soft goat's cheese and milk gel

Bring the milk and the agar agar to the boil while whisking. Continue whisking for one minute after it has reached boiling point. Pour the liquid into a tray and set in the fridge for an hour.

Blend the goat's cheese until soft and smooth. Add the set gel and blend until smooth. Season with salt and pepper.

Masala buttermilk

In a hot saucepan with a bit of olive oil, sweat the onion and shallot with the garlic, thyme and bay leaf. Add the masala spice and cook out. Add the buttermilk and reduce by one-third. Blend until smooth and strain throught a fine sieve.

Masala foam

Reduce the cream by half. Sweat the onion and shallot with the crushed garlic, thyme and bay leaf in a saucepan. Add the masala spice and cook out to get all the fragance of the spices. Add the chicken stock, reduce by half and blend. Strain the masala liquid into the reduced cream. Add lecithin and bring to the boil.

Masala nuts

Heat a frying pan to medium temperature. Toast hazelnuts in the oven at 200°C for four minutes. Place the nuts and the masala in the heated pan and shake for five to 10 seconds. Remove onto a tray to cool down. Blend half of the nuts slightly into a rough crumble.
Serves 4

Reuben's at the Robertson Small Hotel

Asian-infused, country-inspired and ever-changing

The Robertson Small Hotel,
58 Van Reenen Street,
Robertson, 6705
+27 23 626 7200 for
reservations (essential)
www.therobertsonsmallhotel.com
GPS: S33°48'00.40"
E19°52'46.90"

Robertson is a small, tight-knit town in the Breede River Valley, slowly edging its way onto the culinary map. Small is not the first word that comes to mind when reliving a stay at the Robertson Small Hotel. Here they are big on attention to detail, with warm and friendly service. Boasting 10 en-suite luxury rooms with five that open onto the pool, they have earned their five-star status. The sixth star is the chef, working wonders in Reuben's restaurant.

Tiaan van Greunen is playful and professional. Hailing from another small town, Oudtshoorn, he originally earned his stripes at Reuben Riffel's original restaurant in Franschhoek. This intimate restaurant is providing a platform for him to explore his own passion and creativity, yet retain his essence of

being a country person who supports local farmers. He sources exotic vegetables grown locally by producers who source seeds internationally, and often the menu changes to accommodate a new ingredient. He claims to combine what people want with what is being produced and, being a sports-lover, pays attention to nutritional value too.

'My inspiration comes from the love of making the food. I think that is the first rule that matters if you want to create a dish. I look in books and on apps and then make it my own. It helps to go and eat at different places with different styles of food and that's also how you catch up on the new food trends. I love herbs and spices. Think about what flavour you want in that dish and pick your herbs and spices accordingly, without adding too much of any ingredient. You want to find that balance.'

"My inspiration comes from the love of making the food. I think that is the first rule that matters if you want to create a dish."

Chef Tiaan van Greunen

Tiaan's cuisine is fresh and full of surprises. 'Because Asian foods are often sweet, we need to get that perfect balance between acidity and sweetness. Mixing the two together and seeing the end result is just amazing. I play a lot with flavours and tastes in the dessert section. Food tastes better and it looks better when it's in season. I only use seasonal products, but being in Robertson it's sometimes difficult to get everything that I want.'

The eclectic and innovative menu changes seasonally, and winter sees a focus on heartier comfort food. Tiaan's number one dish is Norwegian salmon, accompanied by a glass of rosé brut. He is yet another chef who supports the South African braai!

The cuisine inspired by renowned TV chef Reuben Riffel can also be enjoyed at Reuben's in the V&A Waterfront (in the sumptuous One&Only Hotel), the culinary street of Franschhoek, or in the seaside village of Paternoster.

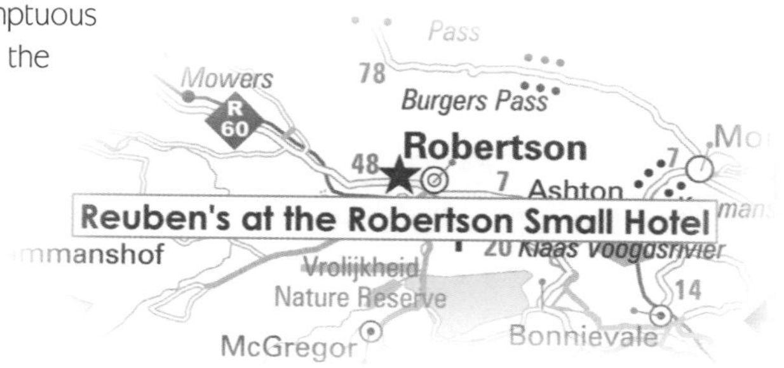

Pork belly

INGREDIENTS

Date purée

250g dates

Kimchi spice mix

30g ginger, peeled and sliced
30g garlic, peeled
8g dried shrimp, lightly toasted and roughly chopped
50g tamari
60g fish sauce
40g chilli powder (togarashi)
120g sugar

Kimchi

400g Chinese cabbage
600g red cabbage
15g flaky sea salt
15g castor sugar
40g spring onions, thickly sliced
50g carrots, peeled and julienned
kimchi spice mix

Potato croquettes

2 tablespoons milk
salt to taste
½ teaspoon pepper
1 onion, chopped
2 tablespoons chopped fresh coriander
2 egg yolks, beaten
3 tablespoons flour
4 cups mashed potatoes
1 egg, beaten
sifted dried breadcrumbs

Pink peppercorn-caramel sauce

¼ cup palm sugar
¼ cup water
2 tablespoons crushed ginger
4 tablespoons Thai fish sauce
zest and juice of 1 orange
¼ cup pink peppercorns

Pork belly

500g pork belly, whole and bone in
2 cups chicken stock
peel of 1 orange
1 cup soy sauce
1 small piece fresh ginger, peeled and chopped
1 star anise
1 small cinnamon stick
½ cup sugar

To serve

Brussels sprouts
peeled and sliced orange
lemon quarters

METHOD

Date purée

Pit the dates and remove any bits of stem. Place the dates in a pan, cover with water and simmer until soft, for about 10 minutes. Once the dates are soft, remove from heat. Allow to cool, then place the water and dates in a blender and blend until smooth. Strain through a chinois.

Kimchi spice mix

Blitz together all of the ingredients in a small food processor.

Kimchi

Chiffonade the Chinese and red cabbages and place in a bowl. Vigorously rub in the salt and the sugar and leave overnight in the fridge. Squeeze any excess liquid from the cabbage mix and combine with the spring onions, carrots and kimchi spice mix.

Potato croquettes

Add milk, salt, pepper, chopped onion, coriander, beaten egg yolks and flour to mashed potatoes. Roll into balls and dip in the beaten egg, then roll through breadcrumbs. Deep-fry.

Pink peppercorn-caramel sauce

In a saucepan, bring the palm sugar and water to the boil. Simmer until mixture starts to caramelise. Add the remaining ingredients and simmer on low heat for two minutes.

Pork belly

Preheat the oven to 160°C. Place pork belly in a small oven tray, to fit snugly. Mix together the stock, orange peel, soy sauce, ginger, star anise, cinnamon stick and sugar and stir well. Cover the pork with the mixture and cover the oven tray with tinfoil. Roast in the oven for four hours. Transfer the pork to another tray. Remove the bones. Place a similar sized tray on top of the pork and place a brick or other weight (about 3kg) on top of the tray. Leave in the fridge for three hours or until completely cooled. Remove the pork and cut into serving sizes. Roast for 10 minutes.

TO SERVE

Serve the pork with Brussels sprouts, sliced orange, kimchi, date purée, potato croquettes, lemon quarters and pink peppercorn-caramel sauce.

Roots

modern French cuisine inspired by Africa

"Roots makes excellent use of the setting, allowing guests to eat alfresco on the deck, or inside where the views are still sublime."

Open your car windows and enjoy escaping from the city at your arrival at Forum Homini, in the Cradle of Humankind. Mother Nature welcomes you with a soft breeze to blow the city cobwebs away. If you are lucky, you may have a sighting of zebra and springbok as you approach the hotel and restaurant on the dusty road. The quirky cave-style suite accommodation (some call it 'cave chic', others 'very Flintstone'!) affords all-embracing views of the veld and lake. Roots makes excellent use of the setting, allowing guests to eat alfresco on the deck, or inside where the views are still sublime. Its palette of beige with just one wall of colour is soothing and welcoming. Crisp white linen, timeless white crockery and the occasional black slate forms the backdrop for exquisitely presented plates of deliciousness. The food, setting and service are all on a par – in a nutshell, superlative. Expect a sommelier who is attentive and interesting, and service that is equally smart and well timed.

Executive chef Chris Tustian* makes the most of what is in season to craft set menus that are fresh and local. Food is in this British chef's blood, and having followed his heart to this country, he certainly laid down his own roots, always respecting the origin of ingredients. His food is experimental and innovative – well-chosen ingredients, such as game, duck, plants and fruits, that allow the essence of each to shine through, paying homage to the heritage of the area. Look out for the crispy pig ear salad with beetroot dauphinoise, parsnip purée and smoked beetroot gel, or the Chocolate Experience. This chocolate dessert with a gentle swipe of peppermint will make any day feel celebratory, as does the printed keepsake menu, a menu that changes daily and never ceases to amaze.

Chris's favourite dish on the menu is the Halibut, a 'comfy' dish with warm curry flavours and some nuttiness. 'There is not really a specific cuisine that describes us – it's self-combined with the influence of Africa and a bit of French cuisine. It depends on the idea at that stage; everyone in the kitchen throws ideas around. Someone starts and the next person contributes to make it into something very special.'

Breakfast has five courses, lunch four and the dinner is a six-course adventure, for which the wine pairing of teasers makes it extra special. Brunch is also an option.

Letamo Game Estate,
R540, Kromdraai,
Johannesburg, 1739
+27 11 668 7000
www.forumhomini.com/rootsrestaurant/dining-concept
GPS: S26°01'32.01"
E27°45'55.80"

*At the time of going to press, Chris had left Roots, but his legacy lives on.

INGREDIENTS

Mascarpone and beetroot terrine (makes 60 portions)

200ml cream
100g icing sugar
20 gelatine leaves, soaked
10ml vanilla essence
800ml mascarpone
1 litre beetroot juice
50g sugar

Watercress purée (makes 500ml)

1kg watercress

Watercress sponge (makes 50)

450g eggs
50g flour
75g ground almonds
225g isomalt
17g olive oil
200ml watercress purée

Beetroot chips (makes 10–15)

1 beetroot
200g sugar
200ml water

Yoghurt (makes 60 portions)

3 litres yoghurt
30 gelatine leaves

Beetroot sorbet (makes 20 portions)

1 1/3 cups beetroot juice
2/3 cup sugar
1 tablespoon cornflour
1 gelatine leaf

Red velvet sponge (makes 25–30 muffins)

2 cups flour
1 1/2 cups sugar
5g cocoa powder
1 teaspoon baking powder
1 teaspoon bicarbonate of soda
1 cup buttermilk
1/2 cup oil
5 eggs
red food colouring

Beetroot gel (use three dots per plate)

200ml beetroot juice
10ml sugar
3.5ml agar agar

METHOD

Mascarpone and beetroot terrine

Heat cream and sugar, remove from heat, add 10 of the gelatine leaves, the vanilla essence and mascarpone. In a separate saucepan, heat beetroot juice and sugar. Remove from heat after it has boiled and add the remaining 10 gelatine leaves. Pour half the beetroot jelly into a clingwrap-lined deep tray and let it set in the fridge. After it has set, pour in half the mascarpone mix and let it set. Follow the above step once more. Once all has set, cut into 1cm x 4cm slices.

Watercress purée

Blanch watercress in water till stems are cooked. Strain and blend until smooth, then pass through a sieve into a bowl on an ice bath. Pour into a squeeze bottle.

Watercress sponge

Blend all ingredients together until smooth. Pour into a cream charger, squirt up to halfway into paper coffee cups and bake in microwave for one minute. Remove from cup and break into six pieces, of which you will use three pieces on a plate.

Beetroot chips

Slice beetroot very thinly into round chips. Heat sugar and water, dip beetroot slices in the syrup and place on a tray lined with greaseproof paper. Leave in the oven overnight, at 100°C, turn over and leave overnight again.

Yoghurt

Melt soaked gelatine leaves and some yoghurt in double boiler, then add this mix to the remaining yoghurt, making sure it mixes in well. Pour into a clingwrap-lined deep dish and let it set. Quenelle the yoghurt (use a hot spoon to press it into the set yoghurt, straight down to the bottom, twist in a circular motion, and pull it up to form a quenelle).

Beetroot sorbet

Bring the juice, sugar and cornflour to the boil, remove from heat and add soaked gelatine, mixing well. Freeze, then churn in an ice-cream machine. Use a hot spoon to quenelle the sorbet.

Red velvet sponge

Mix all the ingredients together, and pour up to halfway into a tumble mould. Bake at 180°C for 15 minutes. Let it cool and then unmould.

Beetroot gel

Bring all ingredients to a boil, remove from heat, refrigerate till set, and blend. Pour into a squeeze bottle.

PLATING

Use the positions of the hours on a clock as a guide for plating. On a round plate, brush a line of watercress purée through the middle (from nine to three o'clock). On the one end, place the mascarpone and beetroot terrine (nine o'clock), and on the other end the red velvet sponge (three o'clock). Add the yoghurt quenelle (six o'clock). Place the three watercress sponges (12, five and eight o'clock). Dot beetroot gel, one dot each between the watercress sponges on the plate. Put the beetroot chip in the yoghurt quenelle. Place the beetroot sorbet in between the terrine and the red velvet on the watercress purée.

Mascarpone and beetroot dessert

The Roundhouse Restaurant

getting the taste right and then making it beautiful

"His cuisine is natural, with maximum respect for the product..."

Round House Road,
Camps Bay, Cape Town, 8005
+27 21 438 4347
http://theroundhouse
restaurant.com
GPS: S33°56'37.14"
E18°23'05.50"

The Roundhouse Restaurant commands first prize for position - a haven in the greenery of Table Mountain above busy Camps Bay, with elevated views that stop you in your tracks. In the 1800s Lord Charles Somerset used the building as his hunting lodge. Minimal decor in the restaurant is unfussy, classic and classy.

Chef Dylan Laity spent four years at Aubergine getting a solid foundation before becoming sous chef at the Roundhouse, and a year later was promoted to executive chef. Humble, he claims that the success of the restaurant is a team effort. 'It is my job to stimulate and motivate my team to cook the food that I have thought and dreamt about.' Service is slick and Dylan bravely claims that people are more important in creating a good restaurant experience than the food.

Inspired by his passion and love of food, stimulated by books, the world of food and YouTube, he simply wants diners to enjoy his food, and is not chasing awards. 'We are just doing what we love to do.' When he is not cooking he is surfing, believing that balance, on the plate and in life, is of utmost importance. It clears his head and gives him space to think.

Dylan's ingredients of choice are seafood or anything acidic, and he considers truffles and caviar a real treat. The first three dishes on the eight-course tasting menu really resonate with him. The watermelon with quail egg, balsamic vinegar and aged Parmesan illustrates his creative genius. The watermelon is cooked and smoked, and cooked again to replicate a beef carpaccio, ideal for vegetarians. The salted ostrich with walnut, blueberry, coriander seed and purple carrot comes a close second, and the yellowfin tuna with kohlrabi, peas and gelled bonito stock is equally adventurous.

Dylan does not change the menu for the sake of it, but allows dishes to evolve. He takes advantage of the seasons by brining and fermenting ingredients to change their flavour profiles, and to be able to present them out of season with a different slant. His cuisine is natural, with maximum respect for the product. His eyes light up when he talks about his travels to Asia.

For a special occasion this chef stays at home, chooses to braai and simply adds bubbles!

Try Rumbullion below the Roundhouse, where children can play and parents can relax with the calming view of the ocean over pizzas, picnics and other light meals.

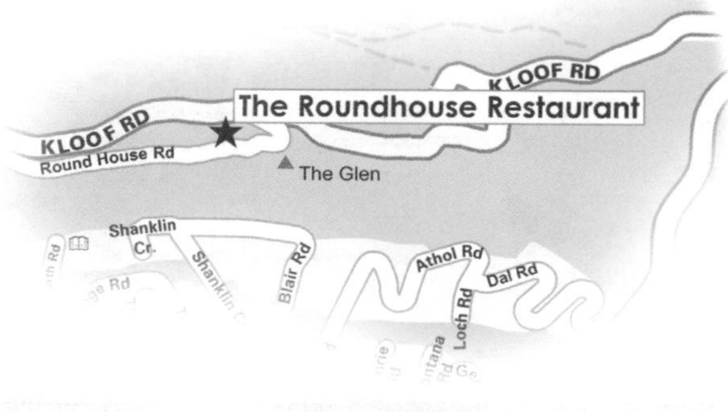

INGREDIENTS

Ostrich
1 x 80–90g piece ostrich fillet
toasted coriander seeds
black pepper to taste
juniper berry powder

Onion and juniper purée
3kg large onions, sliced
30ml vegetable oil
a few crushed juniper berries

Celeriac
500g salt
500g bread flour
water
20g celeriac
10g goat's butter

Cider apples
1 Granny Smith apple
100ml Savanna Dry

Cabbage powder
500g red cabbage
300ml red wine pickling liquid

Onions
3 pickling onions
300ml red wine pickling liquid

Shaved red cabbage
red cabbage

Spiced red cabbage jus
150g butter
200g shallots
30g honey
1g coriander
1g ginger
1g cumin
1g turmeric
1g five spice
1g cloves
2g caraway seeds
2–3 cardamom pods, crushed
2–3 whole star anise
juice of 7 large oranges
juice of 2 large lemons
500ml red wine
500ml duck stock (or veal if duck is unavailable)
3 teaspoons cranberry jam
1kg red cabbage brunoise
10ml sesame oil

Garnish
thinly shaved red cabbage
watercress
wood sorrel
red cabbage powder
onions pickled in red wine vinegar

To finish
15g onion and juniper berry purée
20g piece charred celeriac
20–30ml spiced red cabbage jus
3 discs cider apples

Karoo ostrich with red cabbage

METHOD

Ostrich

Divide ostrich into portions, and marinate in toasted coriander seeds, black pepper and juniper berry powder. Cook sous-vide for 20 minutes at 54°C. Cool immediately in ice water.

Onion and juniper purée

Place the onions into a large saucepan with the vegetable oil and juniper berries, and caramelise slowly until deep golden brown. Remove the juniper berries and purée the onions until very smooth. Season to taste.

Celeriac

Make a salt crust by mixing the salt and flour with enough water to make a dough. Rest the dough in the fridge for an hour, then roll out to about 5mm thick and wrap it around the celeriac. Bake in the oven for about 45-60 minutes, depending on the size of the celeriac. Portion into 20g pieces and char before serving, glazed in goat's butter.

Cider apples

Slice the apple into 1mm thick discs. Cut out with a 2cm cutter and vac pack with the Savanna Dry.

Cabbage powder

Thinly slice the cabbage (1mm thick) and vac pack with the pickling liquid, sealed under full pressure. Cook sous-vide at 85°C until tender (about an hour). Drain the cabbage and place in a dehydrator until it has become completely crisp. Blitz in a blender to form a powder and store in an airtight container.

Onions

Peel the pickling onions, blanch in boiling water for 20 seconds to remove harshness of raw onion, then cool in ice water. Vac pack in the red wine pickling liquid for at least four to five days.

Shaved red cabbage

Remove the stem and slice the cabbage as thinly as possible. Place in ice water to crisp up.

Spiced red cabbage jus

Place 70g of the butter into a saucepan, add the shallots and sweat until translucent. Add the honey. Toast the spices, then crush them to a powder, add to the onions in the saucepan and cook gently (do not burn the spices) until fragrant. Pour in the juices, wine, stock and jam and bring to the boil. Simmer for two hours and add the red cabbage brunoise. Simmer for another hour. Strain, thicken slightly with cornflour, and blend in the remaining butter and the sesame oil.

PLATING

Place one quenelle of onion and juniper purée in the centre of the plate, place celeriac to the right of the purée, and place ostrich (which has been caramelised in a hot pan with 10g of salted butter) in between the celeriac and the onion purée. Scatter shaved cabbage on top, then garnish with herbs. Add the onions and apple slices, and pour the jus next to the meat. Just before serving, sprinkle the cabbage powder over the entire plate.

"It is my job to stimulate and motivate my team to cook the food that I have thought and dreamt about."

CHEF DYLAN LAITY

The Roundhouse

Sanbona

family-style Karoo cuisine

This remarkable wildlife getaway is well worth a visit, not only to see white lions, but also cheetah, rhino, giraffe, elephant, hippo and incredible birdlife. Just a two-hour drive through Montagu and Ashton and there it is, the turn-off to peace, tranquility and authenticity. It is here that one should switch off. The Explorer Camp is for those who want to sleep outdoors in a tent; Dwyka is a series of nine luxurious tented abodes; favoured by honeymooners, Tilney Lodge is more traditional; and Gondwana is for the family. Here, chef Timothy Casten has in his tenure perfected family-style Karoo cuisine – not too fussy for the children but flavoured enough for big palates. His first internship was in the USA as a hydraulic engineer, before he headed to Wales to gather experience in a kitchen or two, one of them under Gary Rhodes, one south of Cardiff in a small hotel, and another in a pub on the Bakerloo line that was originally a slaughterhouse! He worked hard and got good exposure to interesting produce, and also learnt to cook for kids. At Gondwana, the menu changes daily so that guests who are there for a few days do not see the same menu twice. How does a chef get inspiration in the bush? Timothy watches TV and pores through old recipe books, making the recipes feel like new.

Adults and children alike appreciate the standard of quality and innovative toppings (and banting bases) emanating from the pizza oven, and the traditional boma evening. 'I work with what I love,' says Timothy – almonds, olive oil and lamb from locals, plus apples, oranges and strawberries. He has fresh herbs and vegetables in the garden, and he even pickles olives from his own olive trees. Lunch favourites include his venison burger – truly superb. The service at all times from all staff is friendly, attentive and personal. You may be able to view zebra from your room, and the constant presence of birds is guaranteed. Game drives give a pleasing mix of spotting wildlife and learning about flora from experienced guides.

INGREDIENTS

125-175g portion venison fillet
150ml Worcestershire sauce
20g biltong spice
75g pearl barley
250ml chicken stock
10g dried apricots, chopped
30g butter
2 baby carrots
250ml orange juice
100ml water
2 candy-striped baby beetroot
2 golden baby beetroot
100ml olive oil
salt and pepper to taste
1 baby corn
250ml vegetable stock
75g butternut, cut into cubes
50-75ml extra virgin olive oil
1 rasher streaky bacon, for wrapping fillet
toothpick, to hold bacon in place
250ml red wine
250ml beef stock
1 sprig fresh thyme
preserved green fig, quartered, for garnishing
sprig of fresh thyme, for garnishing

METHOD

Marinate the venison fillet in the Worcestershire sauce and biltong spice for eight hours. In the meantime cook the pearl barley in the chicken stock, then add the chopped dried apricots and butter.

Cook the baby carrots in the mixture of orange juice and water until al dente. Roast the baby beetroot in the oven (180°C) with olive oil, salt and pepper for five minutes until a nice colour appears and they are tender. Blanch the baby corn in vegetable stock until al dente. Roast butternut cubes in the oven (180°C) with extra virgin olive oil until cooked, then purée with a stick blender or hand blender. Once the venison has marinated, wrap in bacon and secure with toothpick. Preheat a frying pan containing a little olive oil. When the pan is hot, only seal the venison and then remove from the heat to rest. Once rested, place the venison in the oven (180°C) to continue cooking the meat - this is where your choice of medium-rare to medium-well comes in. It is best not to cook the venison to more than medium, because it tends to dry out.

To make the sauce, reduce the red wine until a nice sticky glaze forms, and then add beef stock and fresh thyme. Cook for another 10 minutes or so on low heat until you are left with 50ml of a nice even jus. To finish off, garnish with preserved green fig and a sprig of fresh thyme.

Route 62 between Montagu and Barrydale, Little Karoo, Montagu, 6720
+27 21 010 0028
www.sanbona.com
GPS: S33°55'09.04" E20°29'54.26"

Marinated venison wrapped in bacon

Springfontein Eats

eat, drink, sleep, breathe

"Their secret to success is consistency, and a top-class chef who makes the most of the produce springing to life on his doorstep."

The sleepy town of Stanford is sleepy no more, yet it remains tranquil and charming with much on offer for the gourmet traveller. Springfontein pops to the top of the 'to-do-before-you-die' list, but doing absolutely nothing on this farm other than enjoying the surroundings and globally recognised cuisine is also an option.

Accommodation in the cottages is rustic yet classy, and this makes the venue popular for special stay-over occasions. The owners of Springfontein, Dr Johst Weber and Jennifer Packard Weber, are rightfully proud of the fruits of their labour. Chickens, herbs, olive and fruit trees, vineyards and organic vegetables – the bounty here is enormous. They have the wise ethos of good planning. 'In Germany we don't just dream, we have a plan.' Their plan has paid off and the restaurant, authentic country accommodation, and five-star cuisine in a relaxed setting allow one to breathe. Their secret to success is consistency, and a top-class chef who makes the most of the produce springing to life on his doorstep.

Chef Jürgen Schneider believes that you should leave food as nature gave it to you. He and his wife Susan have been at Springfontein since 2013. His food is sophisticated and special, yet uncontrived. For 18 years he held a Michelin star in Germany. He has ventured into the world of foraging, and instructs his chefs daily to 'go into nature'. Some of them have qualified in his homeland and come to Stanford to work under this maestro for practical experience. The menu changes daily according to what has been picked and harvested. Wines from Springfontein and its neighbours accompany three-, four-, five- or six-course menus ... with 'greetings from the kitchen' and 'sweet fare thee well' before and after. You may think his springbok with cabbage and sunflower seeds or seafood with peas and curry sound simple, but they are complex and can compete with any restaurant on the planet. The dessert with tomatoes and olives will take your breath away. Make your reservation for Springfontein Eats. Meanwhile, eat, drink, sleep and breathe ...

Their barn restaurant, called The Bar(n), unlike its smarter sister, can be visited without reservations. Complete with straw on the floor, this is where one tastes the magnificent Springfontein wines and can order German-style dishes.

Moore Road,
Stanford, 7210
+27 28 341 0651
www.springfontein.co.za/content/springfontein-eats
GPS: S34°25'38.04"
E19°24'31.26"

INGREDIENTS

Marinated trout

200g mixed vegetables (carrots, celery stalks, white onion)
30g salt
15g white sugar
5 fresh bay leaves
20g freshly ground black pepper
1 rainbow trout (about 800g)

Succulents and dressing

1 shallot, chopped
50ml sunflower oil
100ml chicken stock
20g honey (preferably fynbos honey)
50ml hazelnut oil
30ml sherry or balsamic vinegar
salt and pepper
300g purslane (go and forage!)

Simplest guacamole

½ avocado
1 teaspoon lemon juice
salt and pepper

METHOD

Marinated trout

Finely chop the vegetables (or use a blender or food processor). Add salt and sugar, bay leaves and black pepper, and marinate the fillets of trout, making sure all of the fish is covered by the marinade, for 24 hours.

Succulents and dressing

Sear the shallot in the sunflower oil until translucent, add chicken stock, and reduce the mixture by half on low to medium heat. After the mixture has cooled down, add honey, hazelnut oil and sherry vinegar, and season to taste with salt and pepper. Marinate the washed purslane in the dressing for a few minutes.

Simplest guacamole

Blend the avocado with the lemon juice. Add salt and pepper to taste.

PLATING

With a large spoon, make a thin 'lake' with one tablespoon of guacamole on the centre of the plate. Wash the marinade off the trout with cold running water. Dry it with paper towel, cut the trout into 5mm thick slices and, while doing this, remove the skin. Arrange the slices of trout on the centre of the plate on the guacamole 'lake'. Remove the succulents from the marinade, and place them carefully on the sliced fish.

Serves 4 as a starter

At the river's edge

The Sugar Club

contemporary cuisine that stays with the seasons

Beverly Hills Hotel,
54 Lighthouse Road,
uMhlanga, 4319
+27 31 561 2211
www.tsogosun.com/beverly-hills/restaurants-bars/the-sugar-club
GPS: S29°43'38.11"
E31°05'14.62"

The Beverly Hills Hotel in uMhlanga, circa 1964, is the doyenne of Durban hotels. It maximises its setting, and while there is no space for a spa, guests enjoy treatments on their pool loungers, or under white canopies (that close) on the lawn. This demonstrates their ethos of intuitive hospitality.

Executive chef Tony Kocke, who has a Michelin star under his belt, leads a great team, and the Sugar Club needs to stand up and be counted. His inspiration is gleaned from constantly changing cuisine and the fact that there are always new ingredients available. His favourite ingredients are duck, tropical fruit, garlic and fresh herbs. No surprise then that his favourite dish is their Peking duck. He also loves fresh seafood tapas and, at Christmas time, butter stollen. He loves Asian flavours: 'They are clean and to the point. It also depends on the time of the year; in winter I enjoy slow-cooked beef cheeks with root vegetables. Sustainability is on top of my list – if we can't sustain it, we don't cook it. In my kitchen we only purchase what the season has to offer. It keeps the chef interested and motivated to work with in-season products.' They change their menus every six months, but run daily specials to take advantage of what is fresh and fabulous.

In this smart restaurant with superlative sea views you can order from a limited selection of Nederburg rare auction wines to enjoy with your dinner. Sous chef Sandi Richmond delivers the perfect consommé topped with a gently butter-fried lobster tail before presenting a memorable teriyaki salmon. The deconstructed tiramisu provides a delightful way of ending a lunch or dinner, while the sounds of the sea banish any travel tensions away.

Diarise a Saturday afternoon for the Haute (high) tea buffet, at which pastry chef Jodi will take your breath away. Between meals, lie on your lounger and let the willing staff wipe your sunglasses – their sincerity of service knows no bounds. There is a dolphin bell on the terrace, and a sign encouraging guests to ring it when they see these animals.

Tony travels to the Cape to enjoy one of his favoured restaurants – Chefs Warehouse & Canteen. 'Otherwise I like to eat on my terrace at home. To cook really way-out meals for my wife is very special to me – something that I cannot find in a restaurant.'

INGREDIENTS

Duck
4 x 250g duck breasts

Crunchy mango salsa
400g red onion, finely diced
40g tomatoes, finely diced
40g cucumber, finely diced
80g mango, finely diced
20g fresh coriander, finely chopped
1 sprig fresh thyme, finely chopped
20ml olive oil
10ml raspberry vinegar

Raspberry tears
200g frozen raspberries
40g sugar
10g agar agar

Carrot mousse
200g carrots, peeled
300ml carrot juice
10g ground cumin
2 teaspoons crème fraîche
salt to taste

Shimeji mushrooms
150g shimeji mushrooms
3 teaspoons olive oil
30g butter
salt and pepper to taste
15g chopped fresh thyme

Natural jus
200ml chicken stock
50ml dry white wine
cornflour, if needed

METHOD

Duck
Pan-fry the duck breast, skin side down, for five minutes, then place into a preheated 180°C oven for seven minutes. Remove the duck breast and let it rest for 10 minutes before slicing.

Crunchy mango salsa
Mix the onion, tomatoes, cucumber and mango and add the coriander and thyme. Drizzle with the olive oil and raspberry vinegar.

Raspberry tears
Cook the raspberries with the sugar for 10 minutes, then add agar agar, mixing well. Transfer to a plastic bottle for easier plate decoration.

Carrot mousse
Boil the carrots in the carrot juice with the cumin. When the carrots are soft, strain and blend until completely smooth. Lastly, add a touch of crème fraîche and season with salt.

Shimeji mushrooms
Sauté the mushrooms in a blend of olive oil and butter for two minutes and season with salt, pepper and chopped thyme.

Natural jus
Deglaze the frying pan in which the duck was cooked with chicken stock and dry white wine, then reduce to the desired consistency. Add a little cornflour if required.

Wild duck breast with crunchy mango salsa, raspberry tears, carrot mousse, shimeji mushrooms and natural jus

*"Sustainability is on top of my list –
if we can't sustain it, we don't cook it."*

Chef Tony Kocke

The Tasting Room

2016/2017 Gourmet Guide

edible stories with superlative detail and flavour

Corner Berg and Wilhelmina streets, Franschhoek, 7690
+27 21 876 2151
www.lqf.co.za/restaurants/the-tasting-room.htm
GPS: S33°54'47.60" E19°07'12.34"

Le Quartier Français Hotel in the culinary capital of the Cape, Franschhoek ('the French corner'), draws discerning visitors from far and wide. With good reason, for it's the perfect position from which to explore the winelands – but more often to sleep over in a delightful Auberge room after sampling Relais & Châteaux Grande Chef Margot Janse's innovative and perfectly executed food 'stories'. This award-winning chef composes an African-inspired menu that is perfectly paired with local wines. 'African-Surprise' is an eight-course menu designed to do just that – surprise, and showcase her gregarious and fun personality.

The lightness and lack of formality immediately ensures that guests relax and enjoy the ride. The bright, bold and punchy decor was conceptualised by her brother Herbert. It provides the platform for a memorable culinary journey. Staff are confident, well informed and friendly, instinctively knowing when to step forward and when to stand back. Margot's inspiration comes from working with a fantastic and creative team in a land that is full of inspiration.

Native to the Netherlands, Margot likes to make use of what is native to the Cape, and favours indigenous ingredients. 'We celebrate South and Southern Africa through our food and service at The Tasting Room. I love sour figs, kapokbos, num-num and baobab. The octopus is one of my favourite dishes, cooked slowly with lemon olive oil. We serve it with a flan made from the cooking juices and squid ink. We make sorrel nori by puréeing sea lettuce from the West Coast with sorrel leaves. We dry this out and serve it over the octopus. We then pour a warm cucumber and horseradish consommé over it, which makes the nori collapse over the octopus.'

Margot's cuisine is honest and playful, paying huge respect to beautiful ingredients. She believes that simple ingredients can combine to make an exciting dish, and it is not the most expensive ingredients that should impress, but what you do with them that should take your breath away. Seasonality and sustainability are the core of what they do at The Tasting Room. Their surprise menu is constantly evolving, always surprising. Margot loves change, not for the sake of it but because she never wants to stop being innovative.

Margot also loves going to Bread & Wine restaurant, for long and lazy lunches. 'Neil's food is amazing and he is the best charcutier!'

INGREDIENTS

Octopus
500g octopus tentacles
olive oil

Sorrel nori
25g sorrel
15g sea lettuce
pinch of salt

Flan
125ml reserved and strained octopus juice, oil removed
1 egg
2g squid ink

Crispy quinoa
50g quinoa
oil for frying
pinch of salt

Cucumber water
100g peeled and cleaned cucumber, seeds removed
5g horseradish, finely grated
1g salt

To finish
a few mushrooms
40g daikon, finely grated
16 radish shoots
thinly sliced octopus
lemon-flavoured olive oil

METHOD

Octopus
Vac pack octopus with a little olive oil. Cook in a water bath at 69°C for 12 hours. Reserve the juices which are left in the bag for the flan.

Sorrel nori
Blanch the sorrel and the sea lettuce in boiling water for 30 seconds. Refresh in ice water. Blend to a purée and season with the salt. Spread the mixture thinly onto a silicon sheet and leave to dry at 50°C for two hours, or until crispy. Once crisp, cut into four equal portions and store in an airtight container.

Flan
Preheat the oven to 140°C. Blend the octopus stock with the egg and squid ink, and season to taste. Rest the mixture for an hour to settle it and remove all the air. Lightly grease six shallow silicon moulds. Place a cloth inside an oven tray big enough to hold the moulds and place the moulds on top. Pour the mixture into the moulds. Fill the tray with warm water, halfway up the sides of the moulds. Wrap the tray with clingwrap, making sure it is tight to prevent it from perforating, and then place in the oven for 12 minutes. Leave to cool, then place the moulds in the fridge. Once cold, remove flans from the moulds and cover with clingwrap until required.

Crispy quinoa
Cook the quinoa in boiling water until soft. Drain and leave to dry on paper towel. Once dried, fry in oil set to 130°C until golden brown and crispy. Season with salt and place on paper towel again to drain off any excess oil.

Cucumber water
Blend the cucumber until fine, add the horseradish and salt, and place in freezer until frozen. Place the frozen cucumber in muslin cloth stretched over a bowl and leave to defrost in the fridge.

PLATING

Place a flan in the centre of a warmed bowl, top with a few mushrooms, followed by the grated seasoned daikon and some radish shoots. Place five slices of the octopus on top and then add the crispy quinoa. Drizzle a small amount of the lemon oil around the items. Warm the cucumber water slightly and finish with a pinch of salt and a squeeze of lemon. Do not let it boil. Place a sheet of the sorrel nori on top of the octopus. Pour the cucumber consommé over the nori.

"...it is not the most expensive ingredients that should impress, but what you do with them that should take your breath away."

Octopus with cucumber, horseradish and sorrel nori

"Margot loves change, not for the sake of it but because she never wants to stop being innovative."

Utensils in the Terroir kitchen

Terroir

French influence and technique, punchy and definitive

Terroir on the Klein Zalze wine estate is a favourite for foodies, with good reason. The setting is relaxed and the blackboard menus enough to make anyone's mouth water. Michael Broughton, self-taught, is a truly talented yet humble chef – a natural. He knows that their clientele, 70% of whom in summer are international, want value for money, so locals enjoy winter specials. There is a fine line between over-fiddled and fine food, and he has hit the spot. 'A carrot must look like a carrot!'

The four-course tasting menu guarantees good value. The yellowtail ceviche with avocado, aioli and pickled kohlrabi and the beef tartare are equally delectable. The panko fried mozzarella with tabbouleh salsa, yum. The salmon with soubise sauce and confit pork belly excel in presentation, flavours and texture. The prawn risotto with sauce Américaine has been on the menu since the restaurant opened, with good reason. The chocolate and caramel tart with raspberry ripple ice cream provides a fitting grand finale, and efficient and friendly service is always the cherry on the top.

Michael cooks with what comes out of the ground. In the last decade he has become more careful and aware of sustainability and works hard to source ethical and local ingredients. 'Our entire menu is seasonal; we have to cook what is available, fresh, in season and plentiful. Sustainability is something we have to subscribe to if we want a brighter future for produce in the coming years. It hurts now, but we hope that by restraining ourselves now from overordering, even overuse, we can look forward to still having these beautiful ingredients available for the next generation.'

"Michael finds inspiration by looking at successful dishes, and tweaking them – not embellishing, but improving them."

Michael's favourite ingredients are good tomatoes, garlic, olive oil, basil, custardy desserts and pasta. If he could use truffles on all his dishes, he would! His current dish of choice is the mille-feuille of mango with passion fruit, olive oil and black pepper, but he also likes a sandwich and a pot of tea, often scoffed on the go in his office. This down-to-earth chef favours eating at home or heading to Lourensford with his family for a pizza, or to Burrata at the Biscuit Mill. For a special occasion it would have to be The Test Kitchen.

Klein Zalze Estate,
Strand Road, Stellenbosch, 7600
+27 21 880 8167
www.kleinezalze.co.za/terroir/cuisine
GPS: S33°58'07.25" E18°50'32.29"

Michael finds inspiration by looking at successful dishes, and tweaking them – not embellishing, but improving them. He reads and researches constantly. 'To lose yourself in a good cookbook for a few days is the ultimate pleasure.' His beautiful book called, surprise, *Terroir*, is a treasure. Get one or get there, but preferably do both.

INGREDIENTS

Deboned lamb shoulder

1 small lamb shoulder (try to get a young lamb under 15 months old)
1 tablespoon garlic salt
$^1/_2$ teaspoon freshly ground black pepper
1 tablespoon chopped thyme leaves
2 teaspoons transglutaminase (enzyme-based meat glue)

Lamb jus

5kg lamb bones
5 large onions, chopped
5 large carrots, chopped
5 sticks celery, chopped
5 heads garlic, halved
4 tablespoons tomato paste
3 $^1/_2$ x 750ml bottles dry white wine
5 litres white stock
5 litres brown stock
4 bay leaves
1 bunch thyme
1 bunch parsley
1 tablespoon whole black pepper

Tomato and garlic sauce for lamb

1kg lamb bones (loin bones are best), chopped as small as possible
3 tablespoons oil
12 large cloves garlic, smashed
1kg ripe tomatoes, quartered
250ml dry white wine
250ml medium cream or pale dry sherry
500ml tomato juice
2 teaspoons dried oregano
2 teaspoons tomato paste
2 teaspoons cold unsalted butter
2 large sprigs rosemary

METHOD

Deboned lamb shoulder

Debone the shoulder (get the butcher to do this), lay it out on a chopping board and, using a sharp deboning knife, cut away roughly half of the visible fat. Check the outer layer of fat and trim away most of what you see, leaving a thin layer on the outside to keep it moist during cooking. Try not to puncture the outer skin. Remove the little fatty gland that sits nestled inside a coating of fat (it will seem white and almost creamy).

Cast your eye over the thickness of the shoulder and cut away any pieces of meat that 'stick up' (in other words, trim it so that it is uniformly 'straight' to ensure even cooking. Lay out a layer of food-grade plastic wrap, overlapping two pieces if necessary, and lay the lamb skin side down on the plastic wrap. Season with the garlic salt, pepper and thyme. Using a fine sieve, sprinkle a thin, even layer of transglutiminase over the meat. Start from the base and use the plastic to roll up the shoulder into a tight, round, even cylindrical shape. Tie a knot at each end. Vacuum seal it in a bag at 8 vacuum and 8 seal, and cook in a water bath for 24 hours at 60°C. When done, let it rest at room temperature for 20 minutes, then plunge into a pot of half ice and half water for 30 minutes. Stored in the fridge, it will keep for three days.

You can cook the shoulder using the traditional method and the dish will taste just as good. If using the traditional method, tie the shoulder as above, except use string at about 3cm intervals and sear in a hot pan until slightly brown all over (five to six minutes), then roast in a greased tray at 150°C for three to four hours, or longer if necessary, until it is tender. Remove, cover with foil and allow to rest for 20 minutes, then slice if using straight away; if not, wrap tightly with clingwrap and refrigerate for eight hours to set. It won't be as pink and pretty as the sous-vide method, but will taste just as nice. When ready to cook again, roast gently in a roasting pan, covered, at 160°C for 20 minutes, then slice.

Lamb jus

Brown the bones well; brown the vegetables well. Combine the bones, vegetables, tomato paste and wine. Reduce by half, then add the stocks and aromatics and simmer slowly for three to four hours. Skim, then strain three times: twice through a chinois, then once through muslin.

Tomato and garlic sauce for lamb

Roast the lamb bones with the oil in a roasting pan at 180°C for 25–30 minutes until well browned. Add the garlic cloves and roast for a further 10 minutes, then add the tomatoes and roast for another 20 minutes. Remove from the oven and deglaze with the liquors, scraping up all the caramelised bits off the bottom of the pan. Scrape everything into a saucepan and add the remaining ingredients, except the butter and half the rosemary. Simmer slowly for 90 minutes, regularly skimming off all the fat and scum. Remove from heat, allow to cool slightly, then remove all the bones by hand and blitz/blend the rest of the liquid and solids until a smooth sauce is achieved. Strain twice through a chinois. Add the remaining rosemary and, in a smaller saucepan, gently reduce until a sauce consistency is achieved. Remove from the heat and whisk in the unsalted butter just before serving, after which the sauce must not be boiled again. It will keep for two days in the fridge if well covered, and freezes well without the butter.

Lamb shoulder sous-vide

The Test Kitchen

global cuisine, cutting edge, South African-inspired

"Seasonality is a beautiful thing that needs to be celebrated, but sustainability is a responsibility that needs to be respected."

Chef Luke Dale-Roberts

The Old Biscuit Mill,
375 Albert Road, Woodstock,
Cape Town, 7925
+27 21 447 2337
www.thetestkitchen.co.za
GPS: S33°55'39.93"
E18°27'27.44"

You may have seen culinary maestro Luke Dale-Roberts in operation at The Test Kitchen and The Pot Luck Club in Cape Town, or at his restaurant at the Saxon Hotel in buzzy Jozi.

He gets his inspiration from his craft, from finding a new way of combining ingredients to opening new restaurants. Luke is also inspired by cooking in different places, making the best of what is there, like spices in Durban, returning to ensure that his food is never boring, but always relevant. He describes his cuisine as global, but South African-inspired. 'Seasonality is a beautiful thing that needs to be celebrated, but sustainability is a responsibility that needs to be respected.'

One or two dishes at The Test Kitchen change every few weeks to prevent boredom. He likes to eat at Rust en Vrede, Jordan, Carne and Nobu. Luke believes that 50% of the restaurant experience is food and the other half is made by the people. His open kitchen reflects his honesty and integrity – there is nothing to hide. Take a ringside seat at the counter to witness poetry in motion, the carefully choreographed dance of young chefs creating plates in unison. Watch dishes being constructed, then appreciate each element as you savour each morsel, appreciating the balance of textures, colours and flavours. Love his Asian undertones and surprises of light flavours with a little bite. The extensive hand-picked wine and drinks list will satisfy any connoisseur. Service is seamless, attentive but not over-powering, speedy without being rushed. Diners here are casual and relaxed, losing themselves in lively interaction over food that is worth flying a million miles for, some in the hope of meeting the man, knowing that interaction with Luke would be a bonus.

This pioneer is truly leading the way, having put South African cuisine on the global map.

Herb-seared game fish, red cabbage three ways, apple dressing with horseradish emulsion

INGREDIENTS

Herb-seared game fish

500g tuna loin
50ml olive oil
15g Maldon salt
40g thyme
2 cloves garlic, sliced

Cabbage jelly

150g red cabbage
500ml water
30ml soy sauce
15ml rice vinegar
45ml mirin
9 gelatine leaves

Cabbage powder

250ml white wine
50ml red wine vinegar
45g sugar
500g thinly sliced cabbage offcuts

Apple and mustard dressing

100g white onion, grated
200g Granny Smith apples, peeled and grated
140ml rice vinegar
200ml soy sauce
1 tablespoon brown sugar
20g ginger, grated
10ml sesame oil
2 tablespoons honey

Horseradish emulsion

5 tablespoons minced horseradish
1 tablespoon wholegrain mustard
2 tablespoons white wine vinegar
5 tablespoons soy sauce
2 egg yolks
400ml olive oil

Garnish

liquorice powder
deep-fried chiffonade ginger
liquorice flowers

METHOD

Herb-seared game fish

Light a fire in a wood oven or in a small barbecue. Place a metal grid over the fire and allow it to get extremely hot. Drizzle the tuna loin with olive oil and rub with salt, thyme and sliced garlic. Add a bunch of thyme to the fire to create an aromatic smoke. Sear the tuna over the hot fire, cooking evenly on each side and allowing griddle marks to form. Remove the tuna from the grid and allow to cool on a tray in the fridge. Slice the tuna loin in 1.5cm thick slices to serve.

Cabbage jelly

Slice up the red cabbage and juice it through an electric juicer. Strain the cabbage juice into a saucepan with the water, soy sauce, rice vinegar and mirin. Bring the liquid to a simmer and skim off the foamy residue from the surface. Sponge the gelatine in ice water and melt it into the jelly liquid. Strain the jelly into a container that has been greased with non-stick cooking spray. Refrigerate the jelly to set. Portion the jelly into cubes.

Cabbage powder

Bring the wine, vinegar and sugar to the boil to make a gastrique. Allow the gastrique to cool. Place the cabbage in a vacuum bag, add the gastrique and seal it on full pressure. Bring a saucepan of water to the boil. Blanch the cabbage for 15 minutes. Refresh the bags in ice water to cool it down. Drain off the gastrique liquid from the cabbage and spread out the cabbage thinly on trays lined with silicon paper. Dry it out overnight in an oven at 50°C. Blitz the dried cabbage in a blender to create a powder.

Apple and mustard dressing

Blend the onion, apples, rice vinegar, soy sauce, sugar, ginger, sesame oil and honey in a food processor.

Horseradish emulsion

Place the minced horseradish, mustard, vinegar, soy sauce and yolks together in a blender. Blend to combine. While blending, slowly pour the olive oil into the blender in a thin, steady stream and blend until thick.

To serve

Place the tuna slices on the plate, top with finely sliced cabbage and dress with the apple and mustard dressing. Dot the horseradish emulsion around the plate. Garnish with cabbage powder, liquorice powder, deep-fried ginger and liquorice flowers.
Serves 4–6

A dish from Tokara

Tokara

current Cape cuisine

Helshoogte Road,
Stellenbosch, 7600
+27 21 808 5951
http://tokararestaurant.co.za
GPS: S33°55'03.82"
E18°55'13.62"

"...his classical combinations are elevated with flavourful accompaniments and sauces."

Perched 400m high above the coastline on the Helshoogte Pass in Stellenbosch, with all-encompassing views of the winelands and sea, sits highly acclaimed Tokara. The architecture of the building is the first sight that takes your breath away, an occurrence that will happen often once you are there. Enjoy the art in the garden, entrance and tasting room. The contemporary decor with glass, steel and stone is, like the building, iconic. Have a pre-dinner drink at the bar and sneak a glimpse into the kitchen or slowly watch the sun set. Then let your culinary escapade begin.

Richard Carstens has a sense of adventure which is evident on his elegant plates. Influenced by the flavours of Asia and Europe, his classical combinations are elevated with flavourful accompaniments and sauces. Try his rainbow trout with radish, herbs, cucumber, apple, trout crackling and roast lemon cream. Another good example of his style is seen in the soya-glazed chicken with sushi rice, pak choy, broccoli, pickled cucumber and a coconut tamarind sauce. Finish off with the strawberry and Tokara MCC sorbet.

The wine list offers more than Tokara wines, and is enhanced with good guidance by their sommelier. Daily specials feature on the seasonal menu.

If you are looking for a more relaxed, bistro-style meal, the Tokara Delicatessen is a great option. Equally beautiful setting, a few specials on the chalkboard, or try one of their popular dishes like the calamari and papaya salad, or a flavour-packed burger. Allow time to sneak in a little shopping or wine tasting while soaking up the setting.

True Italic

a blend of the best Italian flavours, rustic and real

15 Bree Street,
Cape Town, 8001
+27 21 418 7655
www.trueitalic.co.za
GPS: S33°55'04.67"
E18°25'18.84"

"He believes that Italian food is simple – a few perfect ingredients simply combined..."

If you decide to eat your way up Bree Street and begin your culinary adventure at True Italic, you may not move any further. A relaxed space with an open brick wall sporting a few football jerseys, this is where Luca Di Pasquale and his sister Natasha have found their niche. They opened their Osteria del Capo before Bree Street became fashionable and was transformed from quiet offices to a hip-and-happening hot spot for good food. Their mother comes from the Emilia Romagna region of Italy, their father from Sicily, and it is this heritage that has handed down true Italian flavours. Passionate Luca can be found in the kitchen while his gorgeous sister ensures warm and caring service.

They have earned a reputation for serving the best Italian food in the 'hood, and deservedly so. Luca's melanzane parmigiana is widely applauded, attracting vegetarians to his soulful space. It is the stalwart on a small menu of simple regional specialities that changes constantly. Most dishes, such as their signature sausage ragu, are worth a second visit. The recipe for his home-made Sicilian sausage, grilled or prepared as a bolognaise sausage sauce, was inherited from his grandfather. While he loves Cape Town and South Africans, it frustrates him that South Africans put too many ingredients into a dish. He believes that Italian food is simple – 'a few perfect ingredients simply combined'. Luca labels fish as his favourite ingredient, and it is this that he first cooks when returning home to Italy.

The wine list sports South African and Italian wines, and there is a selection of Italian aperitifs and digestives. Go for Luca's home-made grappa. Before you leave, grab some quality Italian fare from the deli counter, or venture down the stairs to discover their party venue where small groups have big occasions. Here, in true all-embracing Italian style, people congregate around one large table, like one happy family.

INGREDIENTS

1kg pork mince (65–75% fillet, 25–35% fat)
23g salt
sprinkle of pepper
½ handful fennel seeds
sprinkle dried chilli
250ml red wine
pork casings

METHOD

Place the pork mince in a container and add the salt, pepper, fennel seeds and chilli. Add the red wine, mix by hand and leave to rest for 30 minutes. Stuff the casings with the mince mixture, using a manual sausage filler.

Sausages can be grilled, oven-baked with potatoes and scamorza cheese, or pan-fried in olive oil and lemon juice. You could also use the mince mixture to make a sausage ragu – make a soffritto of carrots and onions, then add the mince, a touch of white wine and some napoletana sauce. Slowly cook the ragu for two or three hours.

The mince can also be oven-baked with penne pasta and béchamel sauce, used to make sausage burger patties, or simply added to gorgonzola to make gnocchi.

Salsiccia ragusana (Five-generation sausage)

A dish from True Italic

View

modern traditional fine dining - more tradition than trends

Check into the very swish urban resort, the Four Seasons Hotel in the heart of Westcliff, to appreciate glorious views over Johannesburg Zoo, and make it a gastronomic stay. Start with tea or an artisan braai-inspired meal at Flames on the terrace and finish with a lazy breakfast or in-betweener at the deli downstairs, called Cellar Door, that is open to the public. The options are endless, but whatever you do, get to the aptly named fine dining but relaxed restaurant called View. Each table is positioned to give you the best view possible, and affords guests privacy too.

Service is slick, not stiff and starchy. No white linen here; instead, contemporary black slate. Start your meal with personally crafted margaritas, maybe the orange and sage or the memorable chilli option, and savour the view, or the art, before your meal takes centre stage and your eye is drawn to impeccable presentation. A quick chat with their chef, Dirk Gieselmann, and you will understand why he loves playing with and changing the menu. He spent his formative food years in France and made his mark at a three-star Michelin restaurant. While his favourite dish is a memorable carrot and organic prawn combination, his hake and beans must be the favourite of many. He may tell you that the fish served in Joburg restaurants is of better quality than in the Cape because here the chefs collaborate to put pressure on suppliers to give them the best. You may agree after tasting Dirk's seafood, like the skate and scallops. Don't leave without trying his double chocolate desert. Go for the à la carte menu, or a three- or four-course food menu paired with wine.

Four Seasons Hotel,
67 Jan Smuts Avenue, Westcliff,
Johannesburg, 2132
+27 11 481 6000
www.viewrestaurant.co.za
GPS: S26°10'17.07"
E28°01'57.55"

Chorizo crusted hake with black beans, calamari and pimento broth with chips

INGREDIENTS

Black beans

1 carrot
1 onion
1 small leek
1 stalk celery
300g black beans
1 bay leaf
salt to taste

Chorizo crust

80g chorizo
50g butter, softened
100g breadcrumbs
zest of 1 lemon
salt and pepper to taste

Sauce

2 red bell peppers
5 teaspoons olive oil
1 sprig thyme
300ml chicken stock
100ml cream
salt, pepper, cayenne pepper and lemon juice to taste

Chips

1 large potato
sunflower oil
salt and paprika to taste

To finish

4 basil leaves
1 bulb fennel
80g calamari tubes
2 tablespoons olive oil
4 portions hake fillet (180g each)
salt and pepper to taste

METHOD

Black beans

Peel the carrot and onion and wash the leek and celery. Soak the beans overnight. Place the beans into a casserole, add the vegetables and bay leaf, cover with cold water and bring to a boil. Cook for about one to one and a half hours until beans are al dente. Add salt only 15 minutes before finishing. Strain the beans, remove the vegetables and reserve.

Chorizo crust

Cut 50g of the chorizo into thin slices and place in the oven at 80°C to dry for about an hour. Leave to cool down, then place in a blender with the butter and mix until smooth. Place the chorizo butter and the breadcrumbs in a bowl, add lemon zest, season with salt and pepper and blend all ingredients together with a spatula. Place the crumble on a sheet of baking paper, cover with a second sheet and roll into a square shape about 3mm thick. Place on a baking tray and put in the fridge or freezer to become hard.

Sauce

Place the peppers in a roasting pan, sprinkle with olive oil and thyme and roast in the oven at 200°C for about 30 minutes. The skin must burn a bit. Remove the peppers from the oven, cover with tinfoil and leave for 15 minutes. Peel the skin off, open the peppers and remove the seeds. Bring the chicken stock to a boil and mix together with the peppers in a blender. Add the cream, season with salt, pepper, cayenne pepper and lemon juice and strain into a small casserole. Keep hot.

Chips

Wash the potato and cut into thin slices with a mandoline. Place the slices in cold water and wash them, then dry them on a paper towel. Deep-fry the chips in small quantities at 180°C in sunflower oil. Season with salt and paprika.

To finish

Cut the basil into thin strips. Cut the fennel and the calamari into cubes of 5mm. Cut the remaining chorizo into small cubes of 2mm. Heat the olive oil in a saucepan and sear the calamari and the fennel for one minute. Add the chorizo, the beans and 100ml of the sauce. Simmer for a minute to reheat the beans.

Cut the chorizo butter into the shape and size of the hake portions. Heat the grill of your oven. Heat a little oil in a frying pan. Season the fish with salt and pepper and sear in the pan for one minute. Turn the fish and continue cooking for another minute. Remove the paper from the chorizo butter and place on the fish. Place the pan under the grill and gratinate until golden brown. Make sure that the fish is cooked through.

Place the beans on a plate or in a bowl, then pour the remaining sauce over the beans. Sprinkle with basil strips and place the hake on top. Serve with the chips.
Serves 4

"...savour the view, or the art, before your meal takes centre stage and your eye is drawn to impeccable presentation."

Winehouse

food and wine in sensual harmony

Ten Bompas Hotel,
10 Bompas Road, Dunkeld West,
Johannesburg, 2196
+27 11 325 2442
http://tenbompas-restaurant.co.za
GPS: S26°07'51.70" E28°01'57.83"

"Here at Winehouse I have the freedom to do my kind of food, the opportunity to play and do what I love."

Chef Johannes de Bruijn

At this central and classy 10-roomed boutique hotel one can forget that you are in Dunkeld West in the heart of the business precinct of a vibrant city. The glass frontage of the double-volume wine cellar beckons. The green-and-white gardens provide a welcome refuge, and the terrace is the perfect spot to unwind at the end of a busy day of meetings. Rooms boast all the amenities and luxuries that one could wish for, with a welcoming masculine feel.

The general manager Danie Pretorius established and tends to the expansive organic fruit and vegetable garden, providing much inspiration for the cooking team. Edible flowers are visible on the artfully prepared plates. There is a subtle fluidity between the kitchen and waiting staff, explained by their multitasking training philosophy. Everyone understands what it takes to make for seamless service.

Dinner is a sumptuous affair from start to finish. Memorable starters include the salmon ceviche and mushroom panna cotta (which one would traditionally expect to see slightly later in a meal). The sea bass and the quail with pork trotters are also declared sublime.

Chef Johannes de Bruijn hails from Cube Tasting Kitchen, an experience which he found an eye-opener and experimental. 'Here at Winehouse I have the freedom to do my kind of food, the opportunity to play and do what I love.' His food is very visual, and when asked where he gets his inspiration, he states that it starts with pictures, especially Instagram. He loves bright colours and combining colours, evident with full flavours on every plate. He leads a team of young, motivated chefs. When asked where he would go for a special-occasion meal, Johannes immediately replied 'It's got to be Cube, it is like going home; but for pretty sensational or a special occasion it would have to be Mosaic.'

The menu is changed quarterly according to what is being harvested in the garden. Edible flowers are used prolifically. Desserts are works of art. Don't miss out on the famous Bee sting dessert, chef Johannes's version of his childhood ice-cream sundae. Your lasting impression will be of a dessert, perhaps with jasmine, perhaps with hibiscus – either way it will be almost too beautiful to eat.

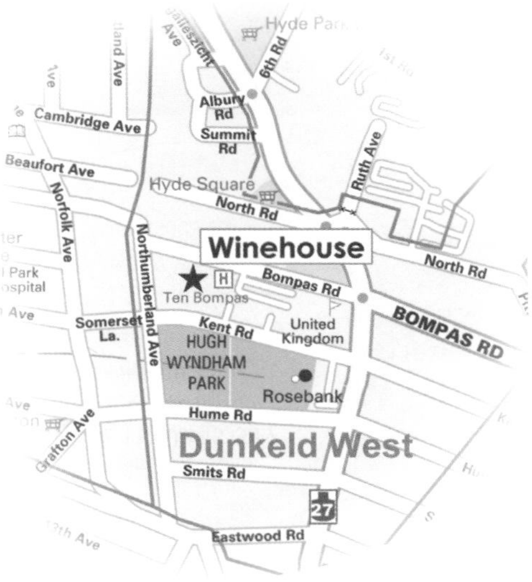

INGREDIENTS

Cherry Syrup

576g pitted cherries
500ml water
50g sugar

Cherry ice cream

500ml milk
100g sugar
100ml glucose
1/4 teaspoon xanthan gum
reserved cherry pulp from making cherry syrup
560ml cream

Cherry cake

100g butter
200g castor sugar
3 eggs
200g flour
4g bicarbonate of soda
10g baking powder
120ml milk

Chocolate ganache

350ml water
400g Valrhona dark chocolate (68%)

Coconut cream

100ml milk
200g cream
500g castor sugar
100g coconut cream powder
80g extra cream

Coconut powder

50g desiccated coconut
40g icing sugar
30g maltodextrin

METHOD

Cherry Syrup

Combine all the ingredients in a small saucepan over medium heat. Bring to the boil, crushing the cherries with a spoon as they soften. Remove the mixture from the stove and cool to room temperature. Strain the mixture through a fine sieve and reserve the solids to add to the ice cream. Return the liquid to the heat and reduce by half.

Cherry ice cream

Combine the milk, sugar and glucose in a small saucepan and heat to dissolve the sugar. Remove from the heat. Place the milk mixture in a jug blender with the xanthan gum and blend on high speed for two minutes to hydrate the xanthan gum. In a large saucepan, combine all the ingredients and whisk thoroughly to ensure the xanthan mixture is blended in. Churn the ice cream in an ice-cream machine.

Cherry cake

Preheat oven to 160°C and grease a loaf tin. Cream the butter and sugar together and then add the eggs, one at a time, while continuing to mix. Sift the flour, bicarbonate of soda and baking powder onto the butter mixture and fold in until well combined. Add the milk and fold in to form a smooth batter. Transfer the cake batter to the loaf tin and bake for 40 minutes or until cooked when tested with a cake tester. Remove from the oven and cool in the tin.

Chocolate ganache

Place the water in a small saucepan and bring to the boil. Place the chocolate into a clean bowl. Pour the hot water over the chocolate and mix until the chocolate is melted. Place the chocolate ganache in the fridge to set.

Coconut cream

Place the milk, cream and sugar into a small saucepan and bring to the boil. Place the coconut cream powder into a clean bowl. Pour the hot cream mixture over the coconut powder, whisking constantly to ensure the powder is completely hydrated. Place in the fridge overnight to cool completely. Remove the cream mixture from the fridge, transfer to a mixing bowl with the extra cream, and whisk to the soft peak stage. Store in the fridge until required.

Coconut powder

Place all the ingredients in a food processor and blitz to a fine powder. Store in a container with a tight-fitting lid.

Cherry cake with cherry ice cream

PLATING

Warm the cherry cake in the oven. Place one portion into a serving bowl and drizzle with cherry syrup. Spoon the ganache and coconut cream around the cake and garnish with cherries. Spoon the coconut powder on top of as well as around the cake, and finish with a scoop of cherry ice cream.

"He loves bright colours and combining colours, evident with full flavours on every plate."

From food to brand and back again

While studying Home Economics at Cape Technikon, Jenny worked part-time for her lecturer, Ina Paarman, who became a mentor and great influence in her career. She graduated with a Higher Diploma in Food and Nutrition. Bewitched by business more than working hands-on with food, she headed up the PR and Marketing Department of Cavendish Square for seven years. She left to open her PR company, JHP, in 1994.

JHP attracted and serviced many food and hospitality clients. They launched many restaurants, including The Big Easy for Ernie Els and Simon's at Groot Constantia. A decade ago the performance division was launched, after co-writing *Raise your Game©*. This life-skills book was endorsed by the Education Department and Jenny ventured further into brand and performance writing and training. Jenny was given her own weekly brand and career column in the *Cape Times*. *Raise your Profile* followed in 2009, with SABMiller as a partner, and Jenny then trained their KickStart entrepreneurs in communication and brand. Her third book, *Raise your Leaders*™, was based on a leadership academy that Jenny facilitated for The Laser Group. Jenny regularly conducts brand training in the hospitality sector, passionately believing that people, and service, define a brand.

During this time, Jenny has become a sought-after food and travel writer, frequently contributing to *Food & Home Entertaining* and other lifestyle titles. She travels regularly to top up her food qualifications with cookery courses all over the world. Jenny has written reviews of Michelin-star restaurants and exotic locations, always centring on how food brings people together and unveils a culture, showcased in print media and in her blog, *Jen's Journeys of Flavour*. 'I travel on my taste buds.' She is a member of the Chaîne des Rôtisseurs, a universal organisation that bonds through gastronomy.

In writing and launching the first truly authentic, neutral *JHP Gourmet Guide*™ in South Africa, Jenny has been able to combine her instincts, experience and insights into food, travel and brand. 'A brand is an experience, given by people. Food plays an integral part of a restaurant experience, but is not all of it. Writing the *JHP Gourmet Guide*™ has been a privilege, not a project. Finally we are able to applaud the chefs of our country, many of whom can hold their own anywhere in the world. Meeting them and exploring their passion has been an honour. It is now my pleasure to pay tribute to the chefs who need to stand up on a global stage to be counted.'

"If you are ever at a loss to support a flagging conversation, introduce the subject of eating."

LEIGH HUNT

Congratulations

The following restaurants have been awarded a rating of one plate – excellent cuisine, a top-quality eating experience:

Restaurant	Page
Aubergine	24
Camphors	54
Ellerman House	78
Hartford House	108
Indochine	114
Jordan Restaurant	116
Myoga	152
Nobu	157
Qunu	182
Springfontein Eats	208
The Roundhouse Restaurant	200
The Tasting Room	216
Terroir	222
Winehouse	242

The following restaurants have been awarded a rating of two plates – exceptional destination dining, extraordinary cuisine that warrants a special trip:

Restaurant	Page
Chefs Warehouse & Canteen	62
dw-eleven 13	73
Foliage	84
La Colombe	130
Restaurant Mosaic	148
The Pot Luck Club	174
The Test Kitchen	226

"Tell me what you eat, and I will tell you who you are."

Jean Anthelme Brillat-Savarin

QR Codes

5 Rooms

Bellagio

Camissa Brasserie

9th Avenue Bistro

Bistro Sixteen82

Camphors

95 Keerom

Bistrot Bizerca

Central One Restaurant

AtholPlace

Bombay Brasserie

Chai-Yo

Aubergine

Bosman's Restaurant

Chefs Warehouse & Canteen

Azure Restaurant

Bread & Wine

Cheyne's

Babel

Bushmans Kloof

De Grendel

Delaire Graff Restaurant

Don Armando

dw eleven-13

El Burro

Ellerman House

Erawan

Foliage

Gabriëlskloof

Grande Provence

The Great Eastern Food Bar

The Grill Room

The Grillhouse

Grootbos Private Reserve

Hartford House

il Leone Mastrantonio

il Tartufo

Indochine

Jordan Restaurant

The Kitchen and The Dining Room

The Kitchen at Maison

Kitima Restaurant

Kloof Street House

Kurland

La Boheme Wine Bar & Bistro

La Colombe

La Cucina di Ciro

La Mouette Restaurant

Le Sel @ The Cradle

The Leopard

Level Four

Luce

Magica Roma

Restaurant Mosaic

Myoga

Nobu

ON19

oneNINEone at the Hyatt

Orinoco

Overture

Planet Restaurant

The Pot Luck Club

Punchinello's

Quentin at Oakhurst

Qunu

Red Chamber

The Restaurant at Waterkloof

Reuben's at the Robertson Small Hotel

Roots

The Roundhouse Restaurant

Sanbona

Springfontein Eats

The Sugar Club

The Tasting Room

Terroir

The Test Kitchen

Tokara

True Italic

View

Winehouse

L'Instant Champagne,
with *Vitalie Taittinger.*
SCEAU DE THIBAUD IV COMTE DE CHAMPAGNE
CHAMPAGNE
TAITTINGER
à Reims
FRANCE
BRUT
RÉSERVE
Reims,
Place Royale.
CHAMPAGNE
TAITTINGER
Reims

BStudio
AN IMPRINT OF MAPSTUDIO

First edition published in 2016 by MapStudio™ South Africa

ISBN (Print) 978-1-77026-848-7
ISBN (ePdf) 978-1-77026-853-1

Managing Director Drew Sherwood
Publisher John Loubser
Editor Thea Grobbelaar
Designer Nicole Bannister
Cartographer Anthony Davids
Proofreader Joy Clack
Reproduction Resolution, Cape Town
Marketing marketing@mapstudio.co.za
Feedback research@mapstudio.co.za
Photo credits © 2016 All images by individual restaurants except the following: Colette Baillie, 36, 37; Nicole Bannister, 67; Corne du Plessis, 73, 74; Nancy Ebert and Kurland Hotel, 125–127; Claire Gunn, 168–170; Jenny Handley, 41; Mickey Hoyle, 62–65, 130, 133; Jono Nienaber, 16, 17; Shutterstock, 58, 66, 72, 77, 104, 112, 113, 124, 134, 138, 186; Dylan Swart, 148, 150; CL Thomas, 208, 210, 211.
Printed and bound by CTP Printers, Cape Town
eBook available from www.mapstudio.co.za and major online retailers

MapStudio™
Unit 3, Block B, M5 Park, Eastman Road,
Maitland, 7405
PO Box 193, Maitland, 7404
Tel: 0860 10 50 50
www.mapstudio.co.za